AIR UNIVERSITY

AIR FORCE RESEARCH INSTITUTE

On the Leadership Journey

30 Conversations about Leading Yourself and Others

José A. LugoSantiago

Air University Press
Air Force Research Institute
Maxwell Air Force Base, Alabama

Project Editor
Oreste Johnson
Dr. Ernest Allan Rockwell

Copy Editors
Sandi Davis

Cover Art, Book Design, and Illustrations
L. Susan Fair

Composition and Prepress Production
Michele D. Harrell

Print Preparation and Distribution
Diane Clark

AIR FORCE RESEARCH INSTITUTE

AIR UNIVERSITY PRESS

Director and Publisher
Dale L. Hayden, PhD

Editor in Chief
Oreste M. Johnson

Managing Editor
Dr. Ernest Allan Rockwell

Design and Production Manager
Cheryl King

Air University Press
600 Chennault Circle, Bldg. 1405
Maxwell AFB, AL 36112-6010
afri.aupress@us.af.mil
http://aupress.au.af.mil/
http://afri.au.af.mil/

Facebook:
https://www.facebook.com/AirUnivPress
and
Twitter: https://twitter.com/aupress

AIR UNIVERSITY PRESS

Library of Congress Cataloging-in-Publication Data

Names: LugoSantiago, José A., 1971- author. | Air University (U.S.). Air Force Research Institute, issuing body.
Title: On the leadership journey : 30 conversations about leading yourself and others / José A. Lugo-Santiago.
Other titles: 30 conversations about leading yourself and others | Thirty conversations about leading yourself and others
Description: First edition. | Maxwell Air Force Base, Alabama : Air University Press, Air Force Research Institute, 2016. | Includes bibliographical references.
Identifiers: LCCN 2016040811 | ISBN 9781585662678
Subjects: LCSH: Leadership—United States. | United States. Air Force—Anecdotes. | Conduct of life. | Decision making.
Classification: LCC HM1261 .L84 2016 | DDC 355.3/3041—dc23 | SUDOC D 301.26/6:L 46/2
LC record available at
https://lccn.loc.gov/2016040811

Published by Air University Press in October 2016
Second Printing March 2017

Disclaimer

Opinions, conclusions, and recommendations expressed or implied within are solely those of the authors and do not necessarily represent the official policy or position of the organizations with which they are associated or the views of the Air Force Research Institute, Air University, United States Air Force, Department of Defense, or any other US government agency. This publication is cleared for public release and unlimited distribution.

Chief LugoSantiago has succeeded in authoring a great book on leadership that is also an easy read. In order to do so, he pulled from not only his life lessons but also his vast experience as one of the most senior enlisted personnel in the United States Air Force. By presenting his leadership perspective in a free-flowing, conversational tone, he has made this writing very digestible for all readers. The authenticity of these critical leadership lessons is readily apparent to even the most inexperienced leader. This book provides an insightful toolkit from which leaders of all levels can benefit."

—Gen Janet C. Wolfenbarger, USAF, retired

Contents

About the Author		*vii*
Acknowledgments		*viii*
Introduction		*ix*

Part 1: Preparing for Your Leadership Journey

1	The Campfire	3
2	Rituals and Instinct	5
3	Inner Civil War, Moment of Truth, and Fork in the Road	7
4	My Green Notebook: Learning to Be a Leader	11
5	That Impresses Me	13
6	Becoming Strong	15
7	Stay in One Place	19
8	Painting Again	21

Part 2: Creating and Inspiring Leadership on Your Journey

9	Raise the Bar!—Reflections	27
10	Troops Talk: Three Actions of Leaders	31
11	Being Extraordinary	33
12	Thinking Styles	35
13	Are Those Steel-Toed?	39
14	I Like Them with a Smile	41
15	"I Have a Dream!" Or Maybe I Don't Have One	43

Part 3: Making Decisions on Your Leadership Journey

16 Self-fulfilling Prophecy . . . The Power of Expectations	47
17 The Job Interview	51
18 This or That	53
19 Watch the Autoresponse	55
20 Thinking Too Much?	59
21 Do the Trick: Troubleshoot before Attempting Repair	61
22 What's Really Important?	65

Part 4: Dealing with Teamwork on your Leadership Journey

23 Can You Teach Me?	69
24 E-mail Warrior?	71
25 My Lego Robot	75
26 The Ground Crew	77
27 Helping Each Other	79
28 Leading Generations, Part 1	83
29 Leading Generations, Part 2	89
30 Building a Space Station	93

About the Author

José A. LugoSantiago holds over 25 years of leadership experience and formal education in several leadership disciplines. He currently serves as a command chief master sergeant at the highest levels of command in the United States Air Force. As such, the he acts as the senior executive leadership consultant, manager, trainer, and human capital analyst overseeing, managing, and developing a workforce of over 24,000 people. In short, he wakes up and labors every day to develop the engine that makes every endeavor successful: people!

He is also an avid writer and speaker on the topics of leadership, organizational behavior, and motivation. His blog, *José LugoSantiago – Craft Your Journey* (http://www.joselugosantiago.com), followed by thousands, features a weekly, provides a fresh perspective on everyday leadership.

The work in this book represents his "boots-on-the-ground" framework of leadership study and philosophy. Although tightly woven in timeless leadership tenets, this is not about leadership acquired in the quietness of a classroom.

What you see in his writing and leadership talks is proven ground in response to questions thousands are asking about leading themselves and others. Regardless of your background—civilian, military, community organizer, or business leader—consider this book your personal leadership coach.

Acknowledgments

I am grateful to the many people who have encouraged me to put these thoughts on paper. Although I have delivered much of this material in my speeches and as I circulate among the troops, no one can deny the power of the written word. It can be shared for ages.

The aim in my work, speeches, and interactions with everyone I meet has always been to make people better—to see them achieve higher success. The special people I acknowledge in the following sentences practice and profess the same calling as mine. They make people better, and they empower others to achieve higher success.

These special people joined me as partners to further deliver a product that can be used by leaders to grow leaders, and by aspiring leaders to grow themselves, and for great leaders to transform their organizations, their workplaces, their families, and their lives. Thank you to all of you for reading the drafts, suggesting changes, and for checking on my progress. All of you are an inspiration to me and the world.

Thanks go to my wife, son, and parents, who were sounding boards during the writing process; Maj Gen Sharon Dunbar, a bright and inspiring leader who knows how to unlock the doors of imagination; and author CMSgt Bob Vásquez, retired, a powerful motivator, my mentor for decades, and the "editor-in-chief" of this work; CMSgt Patrick Wilson, who has been an inspirational leader to me and many others; CSM Donald Freeman, a warrior-leader who epitomizes "circulating among the troops"; TSgt Brad Gurley, my executive assistant and an amazing warrior; and author and executive leadership coach Mrs. Pamela Corbett, whose wisdom has been a guiding light. All of them have taken time out of their busy lives to read drafts and give me feedback. This book is the product of a team effort.

Let us now dedicate this book to all of those who want to serve, and as they serve with fervor, become the great leaders we all aspire to emulate.

Introduction

In early January 2014, I was putting the final touches on this book. My laptop was open, and I was doing some fact-checking. Then, I became curious and asked myself, "If I type 'leadership books' in this search engine, how many hits will I get?"

I went ahead and typed the words "leadership books." The computer's thinking circle came up in the middle of the screen and started turning. Then, the response to my query came up: 504,000,000 results in 0.22 seconds. Wow! I knew the number was high, but that high—504 million?!

There are countless titles out there. Why then would I go on a long journey to write this book? It's simple. I want you to be, not just a good leader, but a great one! I want to enrich your life, so you can in turn enrich the lives of others. Imagine if all of us develop this aptitude and act with this purpose—our world will turn into a dwelling of blessings.

A second reason, perhaps the most unique and noticeable as you read this book, is the framework of leadership from which this book is written. As I was perusing through the titles and authors of the most popular books, remarkably, the great majority of those leadership books were written from the quietness of the classroom and the halls of theory. Seldom were those books discussing leadership principles from the "gladiator's" perspective.

Wait a minute! Since when did leadership turn into a spectator event? And since when did the spectator become the expert in the fight? As Pres. Theodore Roosevelt said in his speech "Citizenship in a Republic," delivered at the Sorbonne, in Paris, France, on 23 April, 1910:

> It is not the critic who counts; not the man who points out how the strong man stumbles, or where the doer of deeds could have done them better. The credit belongs to the man who is actually in the arena, whose face is marred by dust and sweat and blood; who strives valiantly; . . . who spends himself in a worthy cause; . . . and who at the worst, if he fails, at least fails while daring greatly, so that his place shall never be with those cold and timid souls who neither know victory nor defeat.

The framework and point of view, as you and I have a conversation in this book about leading yourself and others, come from decades of my own experience studying, leading, transforming, and mentoring thousands and from success in building leaders and organizations. This is an eyeball-to-eyeball leadership perspective in the arena. Although well-researched and enmeshed with philosophy, this book is about turning a practical experience into a leadership transformational experience. And none of this transformational experience comes from the quietness of the classroom or the halls of theory. This has been developed and proven in the "arena."

These conversations are a collection of my thoughts in response to the questions many ask about leading themselves and others. The conversations in this book are divided into four sections. We start with you (preparing yourself through the cultivation of character and spirit). In the second part, we move into developing influence, so you can create leadership. The third part will help you understand the dynamics of decision making. Lastly, we'll discuss the most important part of your day as a leader: dealing with teamwork.

I am very excited about our leadership journey; consider me your personal leadership coach!

Lugo

Part 1

Preparing for Your Leadership Journey

The leadership conversations in these chapters aim at helping discover and develop the leader within you. Before you try to lead others, develop the leadership power to lead yourself. The first person you lead is you. Therefore, we must start leadership with the most important person: You!

The daily application of the concepts embedded in our conversations aim at making you strong to lead. We'll begin by developing leadership power: character and spirit. Let's talk!

Chapter 1

The Campfire

When your fire is lit, you bring joy to life and help others find their way back to the camp.

One early, cold, and sunny Saturday morning, I went with my son on his first Boy Scout camping trip. He was very excited. I was too. Growing up in Puerto Rico, I remember how much fun these outings were.

Although I did not campout in the "wild" when I was a kid, camping was still an adventure, a fun adventure. When we had carnivals on the island, we used the whole week to camp out right at the beach. My *abuela* (grandmother) made some "nutritive" and really delicious food, and we ran all over the beach. We danced all night while the adults enjoyed themselves.

During Saturday night's Boy Scout camping trip with my son, I observed some of the same things. The den leader and the other adults built the campfire. The kids ran around and played. The adults enjoyed themselves. And we even had a time to recognize the achievements of our young ones around the campfire.

One thing I found curious was the campfire. It was around the campfire that the kids entertained themselves. It was around the campfire that we had our recognition ceremony. The campfire—it was the campfire that made me remember.

I found the attraction interesting. The campfire had this sort of magical connecting power. Just like the sun attracts and keeps the planets in orbit, we kept being drawn to this sort of unexplained power.

I have read many stories about how the campfire was not only the center of inspiration, where rituals would happen in many ancient tribes, but also a beacon of light for hunters who were searching for the way back to camp in the middle of the night.

For me, that campfire also represented my way back. You know what I mean? Well, it was certainly a way back to memories of the past. I could see myself as a child. It caused me to ask a question. Have I forgotten how nice it is to be silly sometimes? I should never forget to have some fun—to just enjoy the moment. Life is a gift.

Thinking about a "way back," good leaders must find their way back—returning to their core values, to what's important, and to what makes them spark! The campfire must always be lit in a leader's heart. As I saw the flames dance and change in color, I searched for my way back, thinking and talking to myself about the importance of keeping my fire lit.

The den leader asked the boys as he was building the campfire, *"What do you need to build this fire?"* The kids shouted many answers. The den leader said, *"You need three things: air, fuel, and heat."*

I thought the den leader's question was a very good one for leaders (moms, dads, military or civilian leader—whoever and whatever you do): What keeps your fire lit? Find your way back. Think through those things that made you spark. Return to those dreams, aspirations, and feelings of goodness.

When your fire is lit, you become like the sun. The planets dance all around you, and you bring such joy to those around you. Stoke the fire. Help yourself and those who are lost find their way back to the camp where you can all be safe.

Chapter 2

Rituals and Instinct

You can reach into the unseen by what you do today. Never neglect those crucial moments of solo repetition and rehearsals. They are the key to your future success.

While on a plane trip, I picked up the airline's magazine from the back of the seat in front of me. One of the pages listed the best martial arts movies ever produced. After reading the reviews, I decided to jot down the list. Well, upon returning from my business trip, I took the opportunity to watch one of those movies.

The movie was based on the actual life of Ip Man, a humble man skilled in the martial art of Wing Chun. His story was compelling—one of courage but also one of dedication. His dedication to a daily ritual of practice, focus, and finding purpose made him strong and gave him the power to defeat adversaries and conquer, with great triumph, his own fears.

I thought about the qualities that made Ip Man successful. The key was a ritual of rigorous practice: hand-fighting techniques practiced over and over again. When the moment came to fight, he just had to apply the techniques. But, after so much practice, those were now instinct.

So I thought for a moment about my observation and how this applies to me. What technique do I need to master so I can be successful? Do I have a ritual of practice that allows me to convert technique into instinct?

During my leadership talks, I'm often asked, "How can I get better at ____?" They're looking for a quick, easy answer. Some people use the Internet to find the latest recipe. Many look for the best thing to buy, thinking this can produce the success they're looking for. Instead, I suggest success (winning) occurs within oneself; what you do in your solo time is the defining factor. It's about how you develop personal rituals and how disciplined you are in executing them. Here are some keys to help you in this endeavor:

- **Get up early.** Getting up early allows you the opportunity to plan your day. It also enables you to put things into perspective early in the morning, when you're fresh and rested. Note: You will be tempted to look at e-mail when you get up. Don't do that yet. Beware of the dangers of e-mail. (See Chapter 24, "E-mail Warrior?" for a useful conversation on e-mail.)

- **Drink water.** Your body needs to stay hydrated for proper functioning. That includes proper functioning of your internal organs but also your mind and muscles.
- **Figure out what's important.** While you're fresh (as you got up early), decide on what is important. Review your goals. Make a list and align your tasks with it as much as you can, so you can execute your priorities during the day.
- **Move.** Get some exercise early in the morning. Exercise can be a spiritual journey, not only will you exercise your body but also your mind.
- **Train your skill.** Take 15–20 minutes to improve a skill. For example, if public speaking is one area you want to improve, use this time to deliver an impromptu talk on a topic of your choice and then evaluate your performance. Or if your interest is martial arts, then do your forms. If it's drawing, then take the time to draw. You choose.

Take the time to analyze your performance. Decide which are the areas needing improvement. Work them into a ritual. Get used to a ritual. Practice your technique. And turn your technique into instinct!

Chapter 3

Inner Civil War, Moment of Truth, and Fork in the Road

Moments in our life's journey transport us to three places. What we do in them molds who we are and want to be.

Can you remember a time where you faced a difficult situation? Maybe it was not a difficult situation, but perhaps it was all about acting on a personal conviction. Did you hesitate? If you did, why?

A rich life is about choosing wisely. We all make life-changing choices every day when confronted with difficult or easy situations. Specifically, every situation you confront will transport you to three places: the "inner civil war," the "moment of truth," and the "fork in the road." Understanding these three places will help you achieve balance, discover who you are, and who you want to be. Let's explore these places through a personal example.

Inner Civil War

While serving on a deployment, the installation commander charged senior noncommissioned officers with fixing a grave problem with appearance standards. (Have you ever been in a place where you thought everyone, and I mean everyone, forgot about standards? That's how I felt in this particular place.) I remember making so many corrections, I could not walk two feet without having to stop someone for something. By the way, with many of these corrections some folks would look at me like I was an extraterrestrial—how could that be?! One Saturday night I decided I was tired of making corrections and the pain of the confrontation process.

On a Sunday morning I got up and went to pick up my laundry. An Airman was standing in line inside the facility with his sunglasses on and in physical training (PT) gear. My inner civil war began.

I went through a series of questions in my head: "What should I do? Should I confront this person?" I really did not want to. Remember, I was tired! But inside of me was this giant telling me to act. I knew it was the right thing to do. After several minutes in line, the giant in me won the inner civil war. I confronted the person and told him to take his sunglasses off. The person stared at me very seriously and, without saying a word, slowly took them off.

The Moment of Truth

Although the above example was a simple one, it reflects several things. First, we all go through the struggle of finding balance in our lives. In the Air Force, we call this balance *Integrity*. Integrity is about striking a balance between what we know is right and actually doing it! Achieving integrity gives us peace, as we conquer our inner civil wars. The example also reflects one more thing: moments of truth.

Those moments become self-discoveries. I discovered, for example, that living a life of freedom was more important to me than being popular. In that moment, I also discovered that I would not give up doing the right thing for the sake of someone else's comfort. I further discovered I had moral fiber and a giant lived within me.

What kind of fiber are you made of? We exercise our will every day in small and large things, but if we cannot discipline ourselves to do the right thing in small things, how will we tackle the large things? We simply will not.

What you do during those moments of truth is important. Notice what you do. Do you postpone tough decisions? Do you seek advice within you, and once you find the truth, do you act on it?

The Fork in the Road

Let me say that the fork in the road is a metaphor. This is the place in decision making where you can decide to go the easy way for the sake of becoming popular or the tough way, risking becoming unpopular but certainly making a contribution and doing the right thing.

In a speech to Air War College students at Maxwell Air Force Base, Alabama, in April of 2008, then secretary of defense Robert M. Gates offered the example of USAF colonel John Boyd to illustrate this place called fork in the road.[1]

The colonel overcame a "large measure of bureaucratic resistance and institutional hostility" to revolutionize principles of maneuver warfare. Breaking through the status quo is never an easy feat for leaders. As Colonel Boyd saw it, everyone faces a fork in the road at one point or another and must decide which way to go: to "be somebody" or "do something."

Those who choose to be somebody will make compromises and turn their back on friends and those closest to them in order to get ahead. On the other hand, others will choose to do something, sticking their necks out for what is right and recognizing that their actions may not gain favor in the eyes of many.

This fork in the road is your last chance in every easy or difficult situation. Whatever path you take, remember that there are personal and social (team) consequences.

If an inspection needs completion and you skip it to be popular with your coworkers (the easy way in the fork), then the mission has been compromised. If you are tough when you need to be tough (the unpopular way on the fork), then you may end up saving a life now or in the future.

Explore these three places. Conquer your inner civil war by exercising integrity. In the moment of truth, discover who you are and who you want to become. And when you find yourself at the fork in the road, exercise your will to do the right thing. You owe it to yourself and those who look up to you!

Notes

1. Donna Gates, "Gates Urges Unconventional Thinkers to Address Unconventional Challenges," *American Forces Press Service*, 29 April 2008, accessed 20 December 2013, http://archive.defense.gov/news/newsarticle.aspx?id=49636.

Chapter 4

My Green Notebook: Learning to Be a Leader

Leadership is never about the critic. It's all about the learning, the reflection, and the action!

As a young Airman, I always had something to say. When I saw a noncommissioned officer (NCO) doing something that was not aligned with my notion of perfection, I was quick to talk with the person.

As you can imagine, I would find myself in several "wall-to-wall" counselings for my "audacity." Sometimes, I just did not have the whole story. Other times, I was immature and needed a clear lesson to understand why. Here is one lesson I will never forget.

During a cold summer, 20 years ago in Germany, I uttered these words: *"Sergeant Jones, I need to speak to the Chief."* The Chief was a chief master sergeant, the highest enlisted rank in the United States Air Force. By public law, only 1 percent of the total Air Force enlisted force can attain that rank.

The particular Chief in question led troops with a stern look and commanding presence. When the Chief spoke, the spoken word miraculously turned into task accomplishment. Lots of power and authority were conferred to him given his years of faithful service, feats in battle, and total military demeanor. You did not speak to the Chief unless spoken to.

Sergeant Jones inquired as to the reason I needed to see the Chief. I told Sergeant Jones I was not satisfied with his leadership, so I needed to talk with someone else. After Sergeant Jones set me straight for my audacity, he arranged an interview with the Chief.

In my unit, I was fortunate to have a chief who was known for his "unconventional warfare" in mentoring young troops. So I prepared myself.

The night before my interview, I got a haircut, starched and ironed my uniform, and polished my boots until I could see myself in them. Then, I rehearsed my speech.

Morning came quickly. I looked sharp and showed up on time. While sitting outside the Chief's door, I said a little prayer, hoping this would not end in another "one-on-one" counseling session, just like the one I had with Sergeant Jones.

I knocked once, as I was taught during Basic Training and entered when told to do so. I stopped at the end of a long table. He was on the opposite side. The Chief looked at me with his usual inspection eye. He could not find fault, so he allowed me to speak.

I spoke to him about my view of leadership and how several of our NCOs were not meeting the standard. He said nothing but looked like he was listening. He reached into a drawer, pulled out a green, hard-covered government notebook, and threw it on the table.

He said, "Pick up that notebook." I did. Then he continued, "This is what I want you to do. [Long pause] Every time you see an NCO doing something you believe does not fit the conduct of a leader, I want you to write it down. Once you have written all over that notebook, and I want more than half of that book filled, you come back and talk to me. You're dismissed."

I was puzzled and confused, thinking he did not listen to my complaints. But I was determined. I kept that notebook and kept my eyes opened to every opportunity. My notebook was almost full, so I asked Sergeant Jones for a new appointment with the Chief.

The Chief looked at the book. I think he was impressed. He perused the notebook and asked me questions when he could not understand my handwriting. Then he spoke.

"Lugo, this is what you're going to do. You're gonna keep that notebook with you. When you become a Staff Sergeant, you're gonna read that book so you don't make the same mistakes. Then one day, you will be Technical Sergeant. You're gonna read that notebook again, and you will remember not to make the same mistakes." Then, he thanked me for the homework and dismissed me.

He never told me what he was going to do. Things changed in the unit, but I am not sure if that was the result of my feedback. He never told me.

Two years ago, I found that notebook as I was unpacking boxes. I perused it and remembered the words of that Chief: "One day you will be . . . remember . . ."

Leadership is about understanding why we do things, learning from others' mistakes, and ensuring we do not repeat those same mistakes. More than being a critic, it's about doing something for the mission, for your people, and for your country.

Chapter 5

That Impresses Me

Knowing is not enough; we must apply. Willing is not enough; we must do.

—Johann Wolfgang von Goethe

The prowess of the leader does not reside in what he or she knows but in what he or she can do for you, for me, and for the team.

I meet with a variety of groups often throughout the month. That time is precious for discussing broad leadership themes, from operations and change management to leadership development to "what's on your mind" topics.

About a year ago, I remember meeting for lunch with a group of first-term Airmen (junior enlisted who are in their first six years of service). The gatherings are always the highlight of my week, and they are full of leadership lessons for me. With decades of experience studying and practicing leadership, an outside observer would think my previous statement makes no sense. Well, it does.

Leadership is an interesting phenomenon. It's not a thing or a person. It's always a relationship between two or more people. Yes, of course, your position in an organization may enhance your ability to lead (or give you positional power), but it really does not make you a leader.

Leadership occurs when two people agree to assume specific roles. One is seen and accepted as a leader. The other assumes the role of a follower. Then, both enter in a relationship bonded by an expectation to fulfill some kind of "psychological contract" with one another.

What makes a person the leader to us? I believe it's the human connection, admiring a set of qualities we end up wanting to emulate because they inspire us and lift us up.

When I started my conversation with our young leaders, I asked them to tell me what they thought. By the way, I did not tell them we were going to talk about leadership. I just asked them to introduce themselves, tell me about two goals, and talk to me about what impresses them. You would love their answers. I thought they were full of wisdom. Here are a few.

"What impresses me is seeing people who are passionate about their work. Those people who give everything they've got and make others feel good. You see it in their smile and their work." (Passion)

"I am impressed by people who can make corrections of others with tact and professionalism. I think one has to be strong to make corrections when someone is doing something wrong. Doing the right thing is being strong." (Integrity)

"What impresses me is one who follows and knows the procedures. I can trust a person like that. And I admire a person that is dedicated." (Competence)

"The strength of an athlete impresses me. It's being strong, to try real hard to outlast the competition, to have the stamina, to win." (Endurance)

"When you have a supervisor that helps you [that impresses me]. I had a supervisor who became my sponsor. He mentored me, taught me about the Air Force, even off duty he would help me. He moved to Incirlik, [Air Base in Turkey], but he still checks on me to see how I am progressing in the Air Force." (Compassion and Caring)

So what's our takeaway? Nowhere in their comments did they once mention position or status. Simply put, if we aspire to be great leaders one day, we must do two things. First, we must continue listening to those we lead. Secondly, we'd better begin to emulate those characteristics our young leaders expect from their most senior leaders: passion, integrity, competence, endurance, compassion, and caring.

Chapter 6

Becoming Strong

Like a rubber band that stretches but then returns to its original shape, being strong is about building and rebuilding oneself.

I've met many people in my life, from all walks of life and many countries, some of whom have made the mistake of misinterpreting what being strong is all about.

Not so long ago, I met one of those people: a leader who wanted to give an appearance of strength and toughness to those who surrounded him. Everything he did was designed to portray that aura. For example, if you needed to see him, he would ask you to go to his office and wait. In speaking, he was impolite. Often he would brag about his impoliteness. I believe that was his way of justifying his erroneous ways. When questioned, he would caveat his comments with, "I am a straight shooter. You want answers, I give you answers—you get what you get with me."

What that leader failed to realize is that strength is internal. He also failed to realize that the seeds of impoliteness and rudeness carry within them the roots of self-destruction. I watched how, slowly, he began to be isolated; no one wanted to deal with him. The great majority of people despised him. Everything he asked was met with just enough energy to produce compliance at best. But really, nothing extraordinary happened in that unit while that leader was there. When it was time for his departure, the people of that unit celebrated.

My point is that physical stature, eyes like an eagle, bold speaking, or an "in-your-face" approach to conflict resolution—none of these things define strength nor make a person strong. Truth be told, the strongest people I have met tend to be the most humble and loving.

History gives us examples of real strength. Take the legacy of Dr. Jigoro Kano, the father of Judo and a philosopher. He believed the most effective way to win over an opponent was not by using brute strength (one's own physical strength) but by redirecting the opponent's force and strength against himself.

We are all acquainted with others who possess real strength. Their stories lift us, inspire us, and make us want to emulate them: for example, Mahatma Gandhi, Mother Theresa, and Martin Luther King. Because they were strong (not physically strong but morally and spiritually strong), they changed the world. We need strong people to do good things in this world. Nature, our own and the one surrounding us, consistently shows us how we can become strong.

Right outside my window, for example, I can see the most beautiful tree. It's an oak tree. This tree is strong and provides my family with shade when we're outside. Other animals and birds live on this tree. I can tell there is a lot of happiness around this tree. The squirrels and other animals play on it every day, and the birds constantly sing from its branches. This tree did not just grow from one year to the next. It has struggled throughout its existence to be what it is now: a beautiful tree! As Napoleon Hill is often quoted, "The strongest oak in the forest is not the one that is protected from the storm and hidden from the sun. It's the one that stands in the open where it is compelled to struggle for its existence against the winds and rains and the scorching sun."

Becoming strong comes from our preparation for life. This comes from the solo work we do in the solitude of our minds. (Remember our discussion in the chapter on rituals and instinct?) Strength develops from the resilience we build when we face adversity—through the act of faith and through the inspiration that emerges when we collaborate with others. These things develop the stamina we need to endure the extra miles of our lives. Let's break those down a little more.

On Building Resiliency

"Do not let the sun go down while you are still angry."[1] This scripture is telling us that we need to learn to let go. When we let go, we can begin to move in a new direction in our lives. Forgive and then move on. The quicker you begin to move in a new direction, the quicker you'll begin to enjoy a beautiful life. It's natural to feel angry at times, but not being able to overcome that emotion will deplete your strength and damage your relationship with others. Forgiving, letting go, and moving on will renew your energy and make you stronger. That's resiliency: being able, through deliberate personal action, to renew oneself and move on.

Resiliency is also about reaching out. Reaching out requires taking risks. The risk I talk about is overcoming self-doubts—to feel accepted or to feel rejected. Reaching out also requires assessing yourself and others. This means learning and acknowledging the strengths and weaknesses in yourself and others. And in doing this, you learn to form strong bonds with people whose strengths can complement your weaknesses. As you become stronger inside, you then become stronger on the outside. This is resiliency and it leads to a more comfortable life.

On Facing Adversity

Don't be afraid of the struggle that comes from facing adversity. Be afraid of not struggling. Struggle in your journey is necessary. It will make you stronger, more resilient, and better able to overcome obstacles in your future.

On Developing Faith

Here's good advice from philosopher and emperor of Rome Marcus Aurelius (161–180 CE): "Everything you're trying to reach by taking the long way around, you could have right now, this moment. If you'd stop thwarting your own attempts. If you'd only let go of the past, entrust the future to Providence, and guide the present toward reverence and justice."[2]

Being strong is about building and rebuilding oneself. It's about developing emotional and mental toughness to deal with others and our environment. It's also about being physically fit—about finding purpose in our relationships. And, it is about thriving in the midst of adversity!

Notes

1. Ephesians 4:26.
2. Marcus Aurelius, *Meditations*, trans. Gregory Hays (New York: Modern Library, 2002), 161.

Chapter 7

Stay in One Place

Don't let your mind wander. Focus your energy. It will improve your leadership and relationships with others.

As I write these words, we approach that time of the year where people begin to think about their New Year's resolutions. Many people come back from the holidays thinking about doing things differently (resolutions). That's good. We should always strive to do better and live better.

I stopped making New Year's resolutions. I begin my year with New Year's commitments! And one of those commitments is to "stay in one place" at a time. Do you know what I mean?

Last year I changed duty stations. My agenda was pretty aggressive: lots of things to accomplish, many places to be, many people to meet. Several times I caught myself trying shortcuts: keeping a grip on my smartphone while in meetings, while talking with someone, or while being with my family. Of course, I can multitask, right? If you would ask me about the net effect of my behavior, I would say there were two effects: misinterpretation of my intent and decreased trust.

There were times when texting someone on my smartphone while also providing direction to the team resulted in misunderstanding of my intent and thereby more work. At home, it was no better. Maybe you can relate? All of the sudden, I was diving into a conversation with my wife about why we moved an event to the following weekend. The response arrived quickly: "I told you last week, and you said 'yes go ahead,' while you were using the phone." Well, I guess I wasn't listening. Have too many of those incidents and your credibility as a leader is destroyed!

There is no such thing as single-handedly multitasking. The brain processes commands one at a time—very fast, but one at a time. The most advanced computer—yes, I am a computer geek—processes tasks one at a time, distributing taskings among processors and often stealing time from a set of actions to give to another, switching back and forth until tasks are completed. It's a law of nature, do one thing at a time.

If you want to increase your influence, I invite you to join me in this commitment: stay in one place. This means enjoying the moment right now, focusing on what is in front of you right now. Bad things can happen when you violate this principle. Let me give you some examples.

When you are driving consider not using your phone at all. A study performed in 2013 by the American Automobile Association revealed there is little difference between the driving safety risks of hands-free versus handheld cell phones.[1] And if that is not enough, a headline in the *Washington Post* back in January 2010 reported that 28 percent of all accidents in the United States involved talking or texting.[2]

If you eat or chat face-to-face with someone, consider keeping electronic devices off the dinner table. Numerous studies have shown how cell phones can hurt our close relationships. For example, in counseling young couples, I have seen how a cell phone became the center of relationship discord. The problem stemmed from the fact that one of the parties couldn't let go of the phone. Even at the dinner table, when everyone could catch up with one another and enjoy each other's company, the phone was present and actively being focused on. Although this particular example highlights phones, the same applies to your tablets, e-readers, game systems, and so forth.

If you tend to let your mind wander while talking to others, consider focusing your energy on understanding and replying, thereby focusing on the person (or subject) in the present. This will improve your relationships and others' trust in you.

Make the commitment; stay in one place. You will improve your relationships and will gain the trust and admiration of all of those around you. You will become the great leader others want to be and want to follow!

Notes

1. Christopher Hart, *Hearing on Improving the Effectiveness of the Federal Surface Transportation Safety Grants Programs* (Washington, DC: National Transportation Safety Board, 2014), 6.

2. Ashley Halsey III, "28 Percent of Accidents Involve Talking, Texting on Cellphones," *Washington Post*, 13 January 2010, http://www.washingtonpost.com/wp-dyn/content/article/2010/01/12/AR2010011202218.html.

Chapter 8

Painting Again

If you invest your time admiring your past successes, how can you move on and seize the future?

Several months ago I read a story about a young Greek artist named Timanthes of Kythnos (ca. 406 BCE).[1] The story reminded me of the dangers of living trapped in past victories: admiring past victories and not moving on. David Cottrell narrates part of the story in his book *The Next Level: Leading beyond the Status Quo*. The story takes place more than 2,000 years ago, when Timanthes studied under a much respected teacher. After several years of practicing and honing his skills, Timanthes finished a most beautiful painting. He loved this artwork so much that he spent days staring at it. No longer was Timanthes painting. One day he came back to admire his painting and found it tarnished with paint. Devastated from the misfortune, Timanthes ran to his teacher.

His teacher admitted to destroying the picture and told Timanthes that the beautiful picture was retarding his progress. His teacher told him, "I did it for your own good. Start again and see if you can do better." Timanthes then went on to produce *Sacrifice of Iphigenia*, regarded as one of the finest paintings of antiquity.[2]

This story reminds me of the times when great people who, because they spend their time admiring previous success, can no longer move forward. Their failure may be due to apathy toward change or just plain fear and insecurity about the future.

A sign that you've been "admiring the painting" too long can be seen in thoughts like these:

"That's not going to work. Five years ago I tried that and . . ."

"I don't see any issues with what I'm doing right now. I think this is perfectly fine."

Or how about this one? "I've been in this _____ (fill the blank with company, unit, etc.) for the past 10 years; we've never had issues. . . . Don't see why I have to change this now."

If you have been doing the same over and over again, it's time to reexamine what you're doing. It's time to see if you need to pick up the brush and begin painting again.

The environment around you is not static. Why should you then stay static? Pres. Abraham Lincoln said it best: "Still the question recurs 'can we do better?' The dogmas of the quiet past are inadequate to the stormy present. The occasion is piled high with difficulty, and we must rise with the occasion. As our case is new, so we must think anew, and act anew."[3]

Your next painting will be better than this one. Begin redefining and improving yourself. Begin by taking the following steps this week. Don't wait for a better opportunity "later on":

1. Become a learner. Using change to produce your life's most awesome masterpieces requires that you get acquainted with different kinds of knowledge. When approached with an issue, learn all you can about it and research its peripheral ties. Question your beliefs about where you are—especially if you feel comfortable.

2. Know about, and begin practicing, these five basic disciplines of well-being:

    - **Physical**. A healthy warrior is said to be invincible. Don't lose sight of your health. Exercise daily. Plan to give yourself 30 minutes a day. That's really not too much.

    - **Mental**. Seek education. Education gives you cultural insight and self-awareness. Take a few minutes a day (either in the morning or afternoon) to read and meditate.

    - **Spiritual**. Connect with your creator. Develop your faith. Spiritual fitness is also part of developing a strong person. This connection will rejuvenate you when things in your life get tough.

    - **Fiscal**. Get your finances in order and posture yourself for future financial freedom.

    - **Social**. Learn about people and connect with them. Form your own circle(s). Begin with your own social interests and slowly expand. Make time to build close relationships, and schedule actions in your calendar: make a call, send a note, and so forth.

These steps should help you develop the power to step up to challenges, however big they may appear. In essence, not only will you admire your previous painting, but you will have the impetus to continue developing several other masterpieces.

Notes

1. H. Fullenwider, "'The Sacrifice of Iphigenia' in French and German Art Criticism, 1755–1757," *Zeitschrift für Kunstgeschichte 52* (1989): 539, http://www.jstor.org/stable/1482469.

2. David Cottrell and Alice Adams, "Set Your Goal: Stretch Objectives," in *The Next Level: Leading beyond the Status Quo* (Dallas, TX: CornerStone Leadership Institute, 2006), 35.

3. Library of Congress, "Journal of the Senate of the United States of America," in *A Century of Lawmaking for a New Nation: U.S. Congressional Documents and Debates, 1774–1875*, 55 (1 December 1862): 22, http://memory.loc.gov/cgi-bin/query/D?hlaw:1:./temp/~ammem_1gdy::.

Part 2

Creating and Inspiring Leadership on Your Journey

The leadership conversations in these chapters are the cornerstone of becoming a leader whose influence makes others want to follow.

A leader has internal power. Remember, power comes from having character and spirit. (That was the focus of our previous conversations.)

But most importantly, the leader has influence, and he or she employs influence as his or her art. This quality distinguishes the leader.

Leadership is the art of influencing and directing people to accomplish a mission or objective.

Developing your influence through your actions will help you create leadership and inspire others to action. That's the focus of this section.

Let's talk!

Chapter 9

Raise the Bar!—Reflections

Commit to excellence. This is the way to improve yourself and others.

A very important and enjoyable part of my week is spending time conversing with people. My aim is to touch people's hearts and minds, see how they're doing in setting and meeting standards, and get feedback so we can reflect.

Headlines in newspapers and events across our communities are examples of the need to engage in meaningful conversations. Most of the time, it's not the positive that is highlighted in the news, hence the paramount importance of meaningful conversations with yourself and others. Those conversations, which later turn into reflections, help us raise the bar and stay committed to the life we deserve—the good life! Here are some reflections to help us raise and meet our leadership bar.

On 27 February 1860, presidential candidate Abraham Lincoln delivered an address at the newly established Cooper Union for the Advancement of Science and Art, an institution of higher education founded in Brooklyn, New York, by industrialist Peter Cooper. In that speech, Lincoln uttered, "Let us have faith that right makes might, and in that faith, let us to the end dare to do our duty as we understand it."[1]

Have you ever wondered why Greg or Sara ended up being busted for driving under the influence, doing poorly at work, or living a life of risks that led to an accident? You may have thought, "I can't believe he or she did that!" Forgetting who one disappoints can lead a person to making wrong decisions. Likewise, thinking about those who want to see you succeed (the "fan club") can keep your actions aligned with the good deeds that meet or exceed the expectations of a better you.

So the question is, "How can I help myself, my family, my people, and others make good decisions?" It all starts with you. Commit yourself to doing right. Doing right "makes might" (gives you power), and that power—combined with faith—gives birth to excellence.

Lincoln's quote, although it speaks about achieving power through doing right, encapsulates the secret for achieving excellence. Excellence is, first, the product of believing: faith. Excellence is also the product of a strong will in action—right makes might! Excellence is, finally, the product of integrity—doing our duty, even when unpopular.

And as we do right, we do right with conviction. Thus, our power increases and our influence also increases twofold. Soon, everything we touch and do transforms into the beautiful picture we had in mind. That's the magic of doing right, of having faith that it works while doing it—the excellent life is born! As British philosopher James Allen posited, "Thought allied fearlessly to purpose becomes creative force: he who knows this is ready to become something higher and stronger than a mere bundle of wavering thoughts and fluctuating sensations."[2]

Someone once told me, "Watch what you're thinking." There is great wisdom in those words. In essence, and as the quote from James Allen alludes, we become our thoughts. Our thoughts are embedded commands, and we give ourselves these commands throughout the day. When we say, "I can't do ____." Then we command our beings to achieve that level of performance. We have just limited our achievement by setting the bar too low.

We can change this dialogue with "I can be ____" or "I can achieve____" or "I can become ____." So what's the effect? The effect of committing ourselves to a new dialogue is a new way of thinking about what we can achieve. This new thinking produces great energy that leads to personal achievements and, therefore, a better quality of life.

If we want our lives to become rich and full of purpose, what do we need to do? We need to commit ourselves to our fan club and ourselves. We also need to commit ourselves to doing right in this world with the conviction that this thing we are seeking will become reality. Additionally, the dialogue we have with ourselves must be different. It must be uplifting and explicit about achieving the impossible.

Part of your internal dialogue should include your own life motto. If you don't have one, get one. The motto below is a good one. One of my students gave me this quote in early 2001. He was a great fan of the Hall of Fame football coach Vince Lombardi. This is another powerful thought. I have made it my own compass and way of living. Lombardi is oft quoted as saying, "Unless you put everything you have into your pursuits, what is life worth? The quality of a man's life is in direct proportion to his commitment to excellence."

Commitment to excellence raises the bar, and it makes for a life worth living!

Notes

1. Abraham Lincoln, "Cooper Union Address," *Abraham Lincoln Online* (website), http://www.abrahamlincolnonline.org/lincoln/speeches/cooper.htm.
2. James Allen, *As a Man Thinketh*, Kindle ed. (Seattle, WA: Amazon Digital Services, 2012), 37–38.

Chapter 10

Troops Talk: Three Actions of Leaders

Despite what we may think, nobody really cares about what you say until those you lead see what you can do.
—Patrick L. Wilson, Chief Master Sergeant, USAF

Often, I ask audiences, "What is a good leader?" From the youngest troop to the oldest, responses tend to be very similar. Questions about leadership (and the subsequent responses) are important. They help us understand what we ought to be. Sometimes what we fail to realize is that creating or becoming "the leader" is a daily process.

This is true in our own personal lives, as well as in our professional lives. We must constantly exercise certain leadership actions until they become part of our nature. Then we become the influential leaders we want to be and others aspire to emulate.

Well, I asked over 300 of my troops what actions make them follow a person as a leader. Here's what they said:

- **Integrity**. This is defined in many ways, but I'll keep it within the context of the follower. This is the best framework to understand what you should continuously do to become a leader. In their own words, "Do what you say you were going to do. Live in accordance with a set of values, and keep your promises." Many years ago I knew a chief master sergeant who was very wise and used to advise leaders, "Your actions speak so loud that I can't hear what you're saying." Integrity is the alignment of word and action.

- **Go the extra mile**. This means you are energy driven to get things done and, more importantly, to set an example of excellence. I asked the troops to explain *go the extra mile* for me. "My leader, for example, goes above and beyond what needs to be done." During the discussion, I affirmed understanding and asked for further explanation. "Well, I mean that this person not only barks orders, but also mentors me when I am having difficulty getting a task done." Going the extra mile also means thinking beyond the task, for example, thinking about actions, reactions, assumptions, and consequences.

- **Caring**. With this one, I responded to the troops, "Ah, the infamous 'C' word: caring. And why is this important anyway? If I need you to take the hill, do you want me to be touchy-feely with you? We need to get things done. . . . I need you to go for it. You need a hug too?!" After the laughter, one of my warriors said, "Chief, I will take the hill. I just need to know you care about me. Then, I'll take the hill and some more."

That's powerful! The truth is that they will do what we ask of them, but if they know we care, their actions extend to loyalty (going the extra mile for us). Loyalty produces followers. A leader without followers is just one more person with great ambitions.

"Ok, warriors, one more question." I had to ask one more. "So what actions does a leader take to demonstrate caring?" I got many responses from them. Here are a few: knowing kids and spouses names, celebrating birthdays, talking face-to-face instead of using e-mail for everything, and—another big one—listening! This is what I call "high touch" and not necessarily high tech.

In short, all three of these "actions" that the troops felt were so important are inward characteristics. They are born by way of developing character. Practice integrity, going the extra mile, and caring, not by talking about them, but by doing every day—that's how you'll develop into the great leader you want to be!

Chapter 11

Being Extraordinary

The difference between ordinary and extraordinary is that little extra.

—Jimmy Johnson

What is extraordinary? On an early March morning, my son and I braved the elements to accomplish the great feat of cleaning and rearranging the garage. It was a mess! As a matter of fact, when I told my eight-year-old son that our project for the day was to clean the garage, he told me, "Uhmmm . . . no thanks . . . I'm going to clean up my room." Wow! He was going to do that willingly--without the constant reminders from mom or dad?! Well, I used some persuasion, and suddenly I had an enthusiastic recruit.

As our mission was coming to an end, I found a round table to put upstairs. "Son, you take the legs of the table, and I'll take the tabletop." He replied with, "Ok, Dad." We carried the pieces from the garage to the house. Once inside, I said, "Son, I'm going back to the garage to get a few things. I'll leave the tabletop here, and you can carry the other parts upstairs." He acknowledged the instructions, and soon after, I left the house.

I came back 30 minutes later. I could not find the tabletop. So I asked my wife, "Where's the tabletop?" It was upstairs, and the table was completely assembled. I was so surprised. With great pride, I praised my son: "GREAT JOB!"

"Son . . . do you know what's the difference between ordinary and extraordinary?!"

He responded, "Dad, it's that thing at the beginning . . . the extra."

"YES! Very good! That's it! It's the extra. Son, you are extraordinary!" I exclaimed.

Kids get it. Adults have to think about it a bit more. I know I do, and you probably need to also. Am I extraordinary? Am I giving a little extra? Or am I just doing what is required of me?

Successful people profess, perform, and give *extra*. There is no success in just doing enough. We do not win championships by just running on the track. We win when we give the extra effort.

The athlete understands the power of effort. He or she knows the pain of defeat and the joy of victory. The athlete knows success comes through giving his or her last effort in the final moments of the fight, even after all reserves appear to be exhausted. As boxing great Muhammad Ali once said, "The fight is won or lost far away from witnesses--behind the lines, in the gym, and out there on the road, long before I dance before those lights."

The truth is that you cannot settle for less than what you can give. Sometimes you don't know how close you are to achieving success until you press some more. Don't give in to comfort. Set the bar high for achievement. (Think about our previous conversation, "Raise the Bar!—Reflections.")

I've seen leaders become complacent and begin to live on autopilot. That's when they lose the *extra* that once made them achievers. Later they can't understand why they lost the "fight."

So what can you do to avoid what I just described and become extraordinary? Here are some of the "commandments" by which the extraordinary live:

- Set high standards for yourself and your organization. And don't apologize for having high standards.
- Be prepared to go the long haul.
- Communicate expectations and listen to feedback.
- Work as a team. Don't push people but enlist them as equal partners in achieving success.
- If the work done doesn't meet your expectations, don't accept it.
- Be patient, be a role model, and be a teacher.
- Praise and celebrate.

Achieving success is the product of the *extra*. Go the extra mile. Give the extra effort. The fight is won every time you expend your last effort—your last strength. Yes, you can achieve beyond the ordinary if you become extraordinary!

Chapter 12

Thinking Styles

Calibrate your internal compass, watch not only what you think but also how you think!

In early 2013 I saw the need to work not only on maximizing my physical strength but also maximizing my mental power. I needed to improve how I approached situations mentally; I needed to change my "thinking style."

Several times I caught myself thinking how this or that task was full of lengthy steps, only to be swept away in a litany of reasons why this or that needed to be postponed for a better opportunity. Ok, I'll give you a simple personal example. Taxes! This is a recurring movie, one I've lived every year. One would think that as a process-oriented person, I would have already devised some kind of natural sequence to get this onerous task done. Well, not really.

Maybe you can relate? All of us have pockets of similar areas in our lives. However, we can't let procrastinatory behavior defeat our forward movement. The power of *now* is much more awesome in momentum than the potential generated by postponing action to tomorrow or a week from now. You need a spark of energy (physical and mental power) to get started, and the rest is all momentum.

The secret to maximizing physical strength and mental power is to change our thinking. Finding the energy to get things done effortlessly is more a function of our thoughts than a function of our physical ability or environment. As philosopher James Allen stated, "Thought allied fearlessly to purpose becomes creative force: he who knows this is ready to become something higher and stronger than a mere bundle of wavering thoughts and fluctuating sensations."[1] The fact is that controlling what and how you think builds a stronger leader within you. This empowerment also helps you achieve goals and, most certainly, overcome the environment.

A colleague and good friend, SgtMaj Craig Cressman, US Marine Corps, calls this phenomenon "mind over matter." As we were talking about thinking styles and their place in personal leadership, he said to me, "There are many stories of poor to rich, weak to strong, and military heroic examples . . . but the cornerstone in many of these stories, outside luck, is thought."[2] Having led Marines during several combat tours in Iraq and Afghanistan, including being responsible for overseeing operations over a battlespace the size of New York City while in Afghanistan, he knows well what thought can do.

"The will to survive, endure, achieve more than we are, start with our own thoughts. Successful thoughts lead to successful acts. Your mind can defeat or propel you beyond physical and/or expected limitations.

"I was forced to face my fears with confidence, and things I initially thought impossible became possible. Every day, we are all faced with challenges. From childhood to adulthood, our thoughts shape the interpretation and perception of these challenges. But then we have to (and we can) make a choice: to dwell on the past or shape our personal reality." This mind-over-matter way of thinking empowers you to become a resilient leader able to adapt and overcome.

In February 2013 I had the privilege of talking with Pamela Corbett, author, neurolinguistic programming master practitioner, and leadership coach, about how I, as a leader, could sharpen my behavioral responses to situations with which I was being confronted. She, too, pointed out the power of changing thinking styles. She pointed out the following:

> Any human experience can be described in terms of its 3 elements: internal thoughts, internal feelings, and external behavior. For example, as you read this, you likely are processing the content, hopefully with interest. "My, this sure is interesting!" That would be your thought which leads to a feeling, maybe curiosity. This feeling then leads to your reading more (a behavior). If, on the other hand, you thought, "This may be interesting, but I've got to get my taxes done," that thought might produce a feeling of worry, impatience, responsibility or something else. Such feelings might compel you to put this reading away and move on (behavior) to your taxes. Just an example.
>
> As in any system, if you change one element in a system, it will impact the other two. So, for example, if you want to change a behavior, change either your thoughts or your feelings. Hint: changing your thoughts is easier.[3]

Pamela has decades of experience doing executive coaching and practical research, so advice like this is wise, full of insight, and, therefore, golden. I often think about her words, and I watch for opportunities to practice what she preached. If I want to change how I feel or how I react to a situation, changing how I think about the situation helps me realize and take advantage of opportunities in my environment.

This is so universal, that no matter what your role is as a leader (chief executive officer or mailroom sorter, sergeant or general, mom or dad, manager or employee), all of us can improve our capacity to do good for ourselves and those around us. Begin examining how you think. Make improvements and continue to develop yourself physically and mentally!

Notes

1. James Allen, *As a Man Thinketh: The Path of Prosperity* (New York: Sterling Publishers, 2012), 37–38.

2. SgtMaj Craig D. Cressman (United States Marine Corps), interview by the author, 5 May 2014.

3. Pamela Corbett (Neuro-linguistic programming master practitioner, executive coach and leadership development expert), interview by the author, 21 February 2013.

Chapter 13

Are Those Steel-Toed?

You will never get the whole picture from a report, e-mail, or phone conversation. Looking at men and women in the eye will give you a good sense of your team and how they are performing.
—Donald J. Freeman, Command Sergeant Major, USA

In our roles as leaders, we are charged with developing and caring for people. This is no soft philosophy, believe me! Some confuse this and think it's about going along, getting along, or making everyone feel cozy. Nothing can be further from the truth.

Developing and taking care of people is about taking one's responsibility seriously and correcting the little things. We know our people can handle the tough and big tasks, but it's in how our people handle the smallest of things that we know whether we have developed a winning team. Do you remember our last conversation? I see some application of that conversation here too, and it is worth remembering: the *extra* separates the ordinary from the extraordinary.

I remember one of those care-for-people leaders. It has been 21 years since I met him, but I still remember my old flight chief. He was not the most charismatic leader, but he certainly was extraordinary. Of course, I didn't think of him that way back then!

Every morning our flight chief was in his office at least one hour before all of us young Airmen showed up to work. By the time we arrived, he had read through the aircraft maintenance logs, sample inspected the toolboxes, and walked the shop to evaluate the job done the night before. And if that was not enough, he had already taken time to get briefed by the night supervisor about everything that had happened while he was away. He was totally aware of mission priorities. Under his leadership, it was not rare to be lined up in some sort of open-ranks formation weekly. I remember one of those mornings, "EVERYONE in the front lab. . . . GET READY for inspection!" So there we were—lined up and being inspected. He would ask each one of us (all 95), "Are those steel-toed boots?" He would check our eyes to see where we had been the night before. That inspection time was his time to look at you, ask about your family, and ask you about the job assignment for the day.

It sounds odd that almost every week he would ask if we were wearing steel-toed boots, but for him, it was important to leave no doubt. One week I was wearing new boots. He leaned over and pressed the front of my boot with his finger just to confirm. You see the steel-toed boot question is about safety, the safety of the troops when accomplishing industrial work in the shop or on the flight-line, and the chief's insistence on such little things kept us performing at the highest of standards—mishap free! I believe we could not have done it any other way. There were temptations, but discipline in the little things kept us from attempting to cross the line in big things.

These are old lessons I take with me every day; the little things matter! Am I prepared to begin my daily duties? Do I look at my troops often? Are they ready with the equipment needed to accomplish their jobs? If I don't walk around and face them, how will I know the answer to these questions?

Boots were made for walking. Get out of your office, look at your troops, look at their boots, and if in doubt, always ask, "Are those steel-toed?"

Chapter 14

I Like Them with a Smile

Here's something little that makes a whole world of difference!

A few years ago, we went on a family vacation with my mother-in-law and her husband. We visited Bavaria, Germany, and it was beautiful: the mountains, the valleys, the traditionally constructed houses—just magical!

Well, for this minivacation, we did as we normally do when we travel across Europe: we stayed in a small *gausthaus* (guest house). When morning came, we went downstairs to eat breakfast. That day, the breakfast salon was packed with guests. Nevertheless, we found a nice area to sit where we could see the mountains, covered by the typical Black Forest trees.

We noticed the waitress was having a busy day—running from table to table trying to satisfy all of her guests' requests. Finally, the waitress came to our table. She greeted us with a very polite but private tone, "Guten tag, was moechte sie zum trinken?" (Good morning, what would you like to drink?)

We all ordered coffee, juice, and tea. She came back with the drinks and quickly got to business. As she was taking our orders, curtly replying at times with clarifications, she got to my mother-in-law's husband and asked him how he liked his breakfast eggs. In his Dutch accent, he replied in German with the most sincere request, "I like them with a smile!"

The waitress quickly realized her behavior and erupted in laughter. We all looked at each other and also laughed. That day, and for the rest of the vacation, she was most wonderful. We always greeted her with a smile, and she reciprocated. I thought we gained a friend.

Can you remember times where a smile has turned things around? It seems like a simple thing, but it truly makes a world of difference when interacting with the people around us.

Leaders need to be concerned with "simple things" like a smile. Why? Because the leader's mood and behavior shape the environment where people work. Years of experience leading organizations and advising leaders in organizational behavior and climate have taught me these simple lessons:

- Toxic leadership behavior produces a toxic work environment. For example, rude behavior on the part of the leader plants the seed that produces rudeness and negativity in work endeavor on the part of employees.
- Toxic work environments deplete the "motivational oxygen" in great people, creating underachievers and clock watchers in an organization.
- An upbeat and inspirational leader produces environments where employees accept challenges and accomplish work with a forward-looking attitude.

Of course, a smile affects the external environment, but rest assured it affects your internal, human environment also. Much research has been done on *smiling* and its ability to help you become a more resilient person and even cure diseases. Here is an example from the Federal Occupational Health Agency of the Department of Health and Human Services: "Smiling can alter your brain chemistry, reduce your stress, and make you happier. . . . Smiling alters your body's chemistry by increasing the amount of endorphin and serotonin that are available to your body. Numerous studies have found that these two neuro-chemicals can help with those bodily changes that you experience as a good mood: body relaxes, heart rate lowers, blood pressure lowers, breath becomes steady, feelings of stress ease, [and] mood lifts."[1]

So there you have it. If you want to make a big difference in the environment that surrounds you and to your own internal being, part of that recipe isn't very costly. Just smile. And practice often by greeting every person you meet with a sincere smile!

Notes

1. Federal Occupational Health, "A Winning Smile," *Let's Talk*, no. 1 (2014): http://www.foh.hhs.gov/eapnews/consortium/smile.html.

Chapter 15

"I Have a Dream!" Or Maybe I Don't Have One

Sometimes the gift you share becomes the powerful force that awakens the dream in someone else's journey.

Last year I picked up Martin Luther King Jr.'s autobiography and reread it. Here's something that captivated my thoughts as I was diving into his writings. This passage is from his well-known "I Have a Dream" speech: "Let us not wallow in the valley of despair. I say to you today, my friends—so even though we face the difficulties of today and tomorrow, I still have a dream."[1] Powerful words, don't you think? One cannot help but understand that there is a call to action in those words.

Let me translate that passage into today's lingo: "Stop thinking about how bad you have it. Don't spend any more time telling yourself how terrible this situation is for you. Let me tell you, although things can at times be bad, I will not lose sight of my dream. I will achieve it! I have power!"

But what if you don't have a dream? I didn't. Some people look at me and say I am successful, but how can that be without a goal or a dream? This is a misconception in leadership. We have been taught that great leaders were the products of pursuing a magnanimous dream. This isn't true in all circumstances. My level of success, for example, although a product of my effort, was, in great measure, the powerful effect of someone sharing their dream of me.

Let me get right to the point. If you want to be a great leader, you need to help others realize their true potential. Otherwise, people may go their entire lives and never realize what they can become. The people you are charged with leading (at work or at home) will become average at best. Taking people from average to great requires awakening or sharing a dream. Let me use my own life to illustrate my point.

I was born on the island of Puerto Rico. While living there, my life was not filled with huge dreams. I spent my time doing what others do: going to school, hanging out with friends, and doing other things teenagers do. Although my parents gave me a strong Christian foundation,

I didn't have a sense of aspiration. Years after I joined the Air Force, I met an amazing warrior, and my life took a sharp positive turn.

That warrior was a well-known person, very respected in the Air Force community we were living in. I was pretty much invisible in that world. Nevertheless, that person took time to sit down with me and get me to read. Yes, read! He taught me the power of connecting with great minds. He also taught me the power of habits.

Habits are a powerful force. That's because we become what we regularly do. If you want to be excellent, then you must do excellent work, excellent deeds, and so forth. That behavior will mold you into what you want to become.

On that journey of vast reading, understanding the power of habits and forming new habits, I developed a sense of purpose in my life. And I started connecting with those around me. Those around me began to be transformed by the spark ignited within me. All of a sudden, I had a dream.

The interesting part of the dream is that it was awakened in me. I can almost say that I became this warrior's dream. He was developing the warrior in me. I did not know it at first, but the dream happened.

Why is that important anyway? In a world where people "wallow in the valley of despair," where the hope of a dream is long forgotten or believed to be unachievable, we can be the turning point.

My invitation to you is to develop your own potential and then work with others to awaken their purpose and to live a dream. Better yet, share and live a dream—that's how you create and inspire leadership!

Notes

1. Quoted in Christine Barbour and Matthew J. Streb, ed., *Clued in to Politics: A Critical Reader in American Government* (Los Angeles, CA: CQ Press, 2014), 65.

Part 3

Making Decisions on Your Leadership Journey

A good hockey player plays where the puck is. A great hockey player plays where the puck is going to be.

—Wayne Gretzky

Leaders make decisions every day. But great leaders make purposeful decisions. This means great leaders' decision making is vision-driven!

The discussions in this section will help you understand the dynamics of vision-driven decision making. These discussions will also help you understand why, and how, great leaders can shape positive outcomes through vision-driven decision making.

Ultimately, you will get good at decision making through actual practice "in the arena" of life, and later through reflection. Let's chat!

Chapter 16

Self-fulfilling Prophecy . . . The Power of Expectations

You were born to win, but to be a winner, you must plan to win, prepare to win, and expect to win.

—Zig Ziglar

While driving from a social function, my wife and I started talking about our son's education and performance. Specifically, we thought about our set of expectations: Are we being too tough? Are our own expectations as parents adequate? Are we expecting too much at his early age?

Years of study and actual practice in leadership and resiliency have opened my eyes to see what expectations do for children and adults. The truth is that the exercise of reasonable expectations produces the same results in children and adults alike. Expectations create self-fulfilling prophecies.

This concept of self-fulfilling prophecy is nothing new. It comes from what it is known as the Pygmalion effect, named after the Greek legend of a highly skilled sculptor who lived on the island of Cyprus. As the story goes, Pygmalion carved out of ivory the most beautiful statue of a maiden. He would stare at her beauty to the point of falling in love. One night, during the festival of Venus, he prayed. The goddess Venus heard his prayer. When Pygmalion returned home, he touched the statue; she felt warm, like a living being. Doubting his senses, he kissed her. The story says that the maiden's face bloomed like a waking rose and her hair shone like gold. She had awakened—stepped off her pedestal and fell in the arms of her creator. Pygmalion's dream had come true![1]

Nowadays, we use this story to talk about how our expectations can produce the results we so desire. One famous illustration of this effect is portrayed in the research of Dr. Robert Rosenthal, who studied the effect of teacher's expectations and its effects on children. If you took a psychology class in college, you probably studied this well-known 1968 research. In short, teachers who thought their students were highly intelligent produced students who achieved higher levels of learning. Teachers who thought of students as underachievers produced students with lower-learning achievements. I have seen this in action several times. It's true: self-fulfilling prophesies occur.

Here's a mini war story to prove the point. Back in 2001, I stormed the streets of Lackland Air Force Base as a new military training instructor (MTI), otherwise known as a drill sergeant. In four years, I trained thousands of recruits in many flights and sections. (A flight is the smallest-type organization in the Air Force. In basic training, each flight is composed of 60–65 recruits. A section is composed of at least five flights.) Among the many flights, Flight 712 is, for me, the classic example of a self-fulfilling prophesy.

When I took over that flight, it was known as one of the worst performers. The previous MTIs (three of them) would remind the recruits every day about how terrible they were. I had fellow MTIs who would assure me those recruits were some of the worst they'd seen and wished me good luck on my new challenge.

On my first day with those recruits, I told them about the reputation they'd built for themselves. And I also told them, "Enough of that talk! It's time for change. You'll live to your fullest potential. I believe it's in you, and it's my job to awaken it." I really cared about those recruits. My own attitude toward them—beginning with my total belief they could rise above their condition—drove me to accept nothing but excellence from them. Trust me; it wasn't easy. But we trained hard, and I reassured them when they needed it. At other times, well, they ended up doing a good amount of push-ups. Those recruits began to believe in themselves and began to ace inspections. Their marching became a scene to watch (chins up, shoulders squared, and steady in the cadence—developing presence as a team), to the point that when they marched, other recruits got out of their way. The recruits of Flight 712 got a taste of success "forged in pain and tempered in honor." There was no way back now. Their last march together was on the parade field during graduation day. They honored themselves by marching during the basic military graduation parade demerit-free, an almost incredible feat.

I still keep Flight 712's picture hung on the wall in my office to remind me of the power of expectations. You have to believe in the power of people—awakening their true nature—then pour yourself into serving them by pushing their performance level higher and higher because you know they can succeed.

We see the same effect in the sports arena. Coaches who set high expectations for their athletes win. Research conducted after the 2008

Summer Olympic Games in Beijing, China, studied factors contributing to successful performance from both the coach and athlete's perspectives. In his research, Bo Hanson, four-time Olympian and coaching consultant, highlighted athletes' comments like this one: "With my coach, we knew exactly what I needed, physically, technically, mentally—our motto was 'Execute excellence.'"[2] The coach's own expectation modified his or her behavior and shaped the relationship the coach had with the athletes. Hanson also noted, "The coach's coaching style varied from being able to be dominant when required, to steady with a questioning, listening approach and two-way communication, to influencing with encouragement and praise."[3] In turn, the above behaviors created strong relationships where athletes felt valued, unique, and important.

After reading and meditating over these thoughts and studies, I felt much better about setting high expectations. Simply put, I should not be concerned that my expectations may be too high; my concern for me, my family, and those I lead should be that I do not set low expectations. After all, people will give you what you expect. Expect low performance and you will get low performance. Expect high results and you will get high results. It's a self-fulfilling prophecy. And it all starts with you!

Notes

1. Josephine Preston Peabody, "Pygmalion and Galatea," in *Old Greek Folk Stories Told Anew* (Boston, MA: Houghton, Mifflin, 1897), 68–70.
2. Bo Hanson, "Success of Coach Athlete Relationships" (Canadian Olympic Study. Athlete Assessments, n.d. Web. 31 Dec. 2013. http://www.athleteassessments.com/articles/success_of_coach_athlete_relationships.html.
3. Ibid.

Chapter 17

The Job Interview

When it comes time to make a decision, do not be misled by "expert" advice; do your own analysis too.

As I was growing up, my dad would talk to me about analysis. He would caution me about accepting the word of experts without the proper use of my own analysis. Here's the funny tale he used to make the point.

Once upon a time, three gentlemen—a mathematician, a physicist, and an accountant—applied for a high-paying job. Each of them prepared, and the day came for the interview. Each was to be called individually and asked the same questions.

The interviewer met the first candidate, a scholarly mathematician with an impressive resume. So after a litany of questions, the interviewer said, "Mr. Mathematician, I am so impressed. You are obviously skilled and very personable. Thank you for accepting this interview. But, you know, I must ask one last question."

The mathematician said, "Yes, please feel free to ask anything you want. What's your question?"

The interviewer said, "Well, I would like you to tell me how much is one plus one?"

The mathematician made a thinking face, and after a few moments said, "Do you have a board?"

"Of course!" said the interviewer. The interviewer made it available, and quickly the mathematician wrote all over the board quadratic formulas, differential equations, and even simple algebra. After 30 minutes of scribing and explaining, the mathematician said, "Sir, the answer is 2."

"Wow! Thank you, Mr. Mathematician. We hope to let you know about our hiring decision soon." And so the mathematician left, and the physicist was rushed into the room.

"Mr. Physicist," said the interviewer, "thank you for accepting our interview. What an impressive resume." And so they went, as in the first case, with the litany of questions and into the last question.

The interviewer asked: "Mr. Physicist, could you please tell me how much is one plus one?"

"Certainly, I can" said Mr. Physicist, and he continued, "Do you have a board so I may be able to explain?"

The board was made available, and the physicist was able to demonstrate how elements of heaven and earth combined their forces to produce effects that were quantifiable. The quantifiable laws of nature were irrefutable, and since they could be counted in chunks of units, therefore, he concluded, "As you can clearly see, the result of one plus one is two."

The interviewer was now truly impressed. He had never seen an explanation like that one. He dismissed the physicist and also told him, "Wow, impressive! Thank you, Mr. Physicist. We hope to let you know about our hiring decision soon."

And so the last candidate was summoned into the room. Finally, the accountant got the interview he was so hopeful for. The interviewer and the accountant went through the same list of questions and then the last question:

"Mr. Accountant, here we come to the final question of our interview, could you please tell me how much is one plus one?"

The accountant stood up. He took a pencil and scribbled in a little piece of paper he pulled out of his shirt pocket. He sat down, looked at the ceiling, tapped the eraser on the table a few times, and asked, "How much do you want one plus one to be?"

The moral of the story?

Surround yourself with experts and motivated people, but when it comes time to make the decision, do not forget to make your own analysis of the situation and then take action after considering all of the information available.

This will prevent you from being swayed by numbers that at times do not reflect the true reality. As a leader in whatever setting you are in (mom, dad, coach, military, civilian—you name it), remember we have developed innate instincts. Trust them. Use them!

Chapter 18

This or That

Lee's army and not Richmond, is your sure objective point.
—Abraham Lincoln

The above quote was President Lincoln's response to Union general Joseph Hooker, who got word in June 1863 that Confederate general Robert E. Lee's entire army was heading north. General Hooker recommended attacking the Confederate capital instead of engaging his enemy, and the president promptly reminded him about the real priority.[1]

Leaders find themselves in predicaments like this every day. Our world offers us plenty of opportunities to lose focus and divide our effort. Our environment constantly pushes us to "this or that." And once you're looking at *this or that*, you will feel tempted to achieve both (this *and* that) or take the path of least resistance. Well, what can I say? Life is not clear-cut, but we have to find the way.

If the leader (and feel free to substitute others for the word leader—father, mother, general, sergeant, and so forth) is not clear about where to go and what needs to be done, how confused do you think the troops (and feel free to substitute children, team members, friend, employees, and such) will be? Overall, how effective will everyone be in seizing clear victories?

An old proverb offers the lesson, "If you chase two rabbits, both will escape."

There will always be this-or-that choices, but the leader needs to be clear on what needs to be accomplished. Clarity and simplicity help us narrow the focus. The clearer your focus is, the sharper you will be.

First, decide what you want and need to do—not as simple as we may sometimes think. The best way to decide is to wake up early and set time aside (when your mind is rested) to determine your priorities. Remember to narrow your focus when pressed with too many alternatives. Regardless of what you're trying to accomplish, the rule is this: keep it simple!

The second part of this advice requires clear messaging. Convey your meaning and instructions clearly to those who are charged with executing. Here are some examples of clear and unclear messaging.

- Clear: Airman, tomorrow, Wednesday, at 1000, at the base theater, we will have Commander's Call. You will be there in uniform.
- Unclear: Airman, tomorrow, Wednesday, at 1000, at the base theater, we will have a Commander's Call. Try your utmost to be there.

There is a huge difference between these two statements. In the first statement, only one choice exists: "Airman, be there!" In the second statement, the Airman has the choice. He or she can claim to have tried but to have been prevented from attending by other priorities.

Although this example is ultrasimple, leaders constantly fail here. If you have a dream, define it for yourself. Then, lead those who are to execute it. Lead your warriors by communicating clearly; commit them fully to the task. Don't give them choices: *this or that* will only make you chase two rabbits—both will escape.

And on your objective ("Lee's army"), seize the opportunity! Don't give yourself up to *this or that*.

Notes

1. Carol Reardon and Tom Vossler, *The Gettysburg Campaign: June–July 1863* (Washington, DC: Center of Military History, United States Army, 2013), 12, http://permanent.access.gpo.gov/gpo37413/CMH_Pub_75-10.pdf.

Chapter 19

Watch the Autoresponse

Instead of telling yourself why you can't do something, think about all the reasons why you can!

In late February 2012, I was in a ceremony commemorating 32 newly selected chief master sergeants. The event was great—largely because of the dedication of the committee members.

I thought for a moment about not only that event but also others I have led or attended. Those events always turn into majestic works of art because the people involved could say, "Yes, it can be done!"

What we tell ourselves and how we approach possibilities shape our attitude, our greatest source of ability. Our attitude makes the difference between getting things done and complaining about why life did not give us this or that. I assure you, the road begins with watching your "autoresponses." Some who have worked under my leadership may have complained to others that I won't hear the word "No." I beg to differ. What certainly drains my emotional energy is having people around me whose autoresponse to everything is "No, we can't do that," or the usual, "We've tried that before," or how about the, "Well, no one has ever done that."

My typical response is, "So what?! Let's be the first ones to go out there and make it happen." Instead of worrying about the many reasons why we shouldn't or can't do something, let's begin thinking about all of the reasons why something should or could be done. As psychologist William James stated, "The greatest discovery of my generation is that humans can alter their lives by altering their attitude of mind."

Let's think about the amazing possibilities for goodness that can be born from doing something that is worthwhile. If the project is difficult, thinking through the reasons we should do it will give us strength. Surely the way will be revealed. The comedian Bill Cosby once quipped, "Anyone can dabble, but once you've made that commitment, your blood has that particular thing in it, and it's very hard for people to stop you."

Here's something many people thought impossible, until it was done: breaking the sound barrier. Man began dreaming about supersonic jets from the onset of flying. As airplanes began to advance, the dream of flying at supersonic speeds came within reach. Nevertheless, many challenges associated with supersonic flying emerged. One of those challenges had to deal with the number of obstacles an aircraft experienced once it got to a certain speed (about 767 mph). Once at that particular speed, it got kind of "stuck"; it could no longer accelerate. That point was later termed the sound barrier. Could manned aircraft really break through that barrier? Another associated challenge was to discover whether a man could or could not endure flight at speeds faster than the speed of sound. All of those challenges and related effects implied that a physical wall existed that could not be overcome.

Experiments with artillery canons, as early as the seventeenth century, were early discoveries of the speed of sound. Counting from the initial flash to the moment men would hear the sound of the canons, men understood sound traveled in waves through the air. These experiments gave way to Isaac Newton's first measurement of the speed of sound in 1687. It was clear that canon-propelled objects could travel faster than the speed of sound, but could a man do the same? The question was clearly answered when Capt Chuck Yeager, USAF, broke the sound barrier. The date was 14 October 1947. The National Aeronautics and Space Administration describes that historic moment:

> Entering this unknown regime [the speed of Mach 0.85], Yeager momentarily shut down two of the four rocket chambers, and carefully tested the controls of the X-1 as the Mach meter in the cockpit registered 0.95 and increased still. Small invisible shockwaves danced back and forth over the top surface of the wings. At an altitude of 40,000 feet, the X-1 finally started to level off, and Yeager fired one of the two shutdown rocket chambers. The Mach meter moved smoothly through 0.98, 0.99, to 1.02. Here, the meter hesitated then jumped to 1.06. . . . At this moment, Chuck Yeager became the first pilot to fly faster than the speed of sound.[1]

Speaking of flying, how about flying without fuel? Pushing through the supposed engineering boundaries, a team of experts gave way to their grand vision. In December 2009, they built a solar-powered plane. Not long after the plane was built, it set a record as the first solar-powered plane to fly nonstop for 24 hours. And that team continues to fly around the world without fuel.[2]

And here is another act people thought could not be done: running the mile in less than four minutes. For years, many athletes had tried and failed to run a mile in less than four minutes. Gunder Hagg of Sweden, for example, established the world record in 1945, finishing the one mile in 4 minutes and 1.3 seconds.[3] Many thought running below the four-minute mark was still physically impossible.

On 6 May 1954, 25-year-old medical student Roger Bannister proved to the world this physical impossibility myth was wrong. In Oxford, England, he established a new record: 3 minutes and 59.4 seconds. This record continued to be challenged throughout the years, with the latest being at 3 minutes and 43.13 seconds, by Hicham El Guerrouj of Morocco in 1999.[4]

These are just a few examples of what can happen when you challenge your thinking and use proper reasoning. When you're confronted with a tough situation, watch your autoresponse. Instead of telling yourself why you can't do something, think about all the reasons you can and should do it. Then, believe, commit yourself, and lead others.

Notes

1. John D. Anderson, "Research in Supersonic Flight and the Breaking of the Sound Barrier," in *From Engineering Science to Big Science: The NACA and NASA Collier Trophy Research Project Winners*, edited by Pamela Etter Mack (Washington, DC: NASA, 1998), http://history.nasa.gov/SP-4219/Chapter3.html.

2. Melody Kramer, "Solar Impulse's U.S. Mission Ends This Weekend," *National Geographic*, 6 July 2013, http://news.nationalgeographic.com/news/2013/07/130706-solar-impulse-energy-flying-plane-new-york-dc/.

3. Encyclopedia Britannica s.v. "Gunder Hägg (Swedish Athlete)," 2016, http://www.britannica.com/EBchecked/topic/251531/Gunder-Hagg.

4. "First Four-Minute Mile," *History.com* (website), 2010, http://www.history.com/this-day-in-history/first-four-minute-mile.

Chapter 20

Thinking Too Much?

Too much or too little info? Don't be paralyzed by analysis. Strike a balance and make a decision.

I got a new smartphone in early 2012. It was a much improved version over what I had—I'll leave it at that! The capability new smartphones offer is just incredible. As I was reading the news, listening to music, and later reading my favorite book on my new device, I asked myself, "Why didn't I do this before?"

Looking back over the past year and a half before I bought that new phone, I can see exactly why the delay happened. Every time I set out to buy a new phone, my wife and I would get information about new telephone plans, new features, and so forth. And so, with analyses of all the new data and available options, we wouldn't move to action.

This phenomenon happens in all aspects of our lives and in business too. You know what I mean? Let me give you an example. In an important meeting, leaders discuss big decisions about organizational changes. One of the team leaders speaks on work currently being done. On the other side of the table, another leader is surprised about the disclosure and replies, "I thought we were passed that already. What are we waiting for?"

All of us are familiar with similar scenarios. Many business scholars call that "analysis paralysis." Although I don't want to offer useless clichés, I do want to warn you about the dangers of too much thinking and too much analysis.

Worrying about having enough information is, nowadays, a miniscule part of the problem. The truth is you need to be concerned with having too much information. Let me give you a quick example.

A study conducted in 2008 (that's almost eight years from the printing of this book) approximated the amount of information consumed by Americans at 3.6 zettabytes daily, about 34 gigabytes for an average person per day![1] Ok, so what's a zettabyte? A zettabyte is 10 to the 21st power bytes. If that does not paint the picture, go ahead and take a piece of paper, write a "1," and then add 21 zeroes behind it. If that does not paint the picture, consider that most computers' hard drive storage today is measured in gigabytes. The next measure is Terabyte, then, Petabyte, Exabyte, and finally Zettabyte.

The amount of information available is just enormous. Analysis paralysis is very similar. Too much thinking, either by analyzing too much or not making a decision because enough data is not enough, leaves you with unaccomplished work. Let me point out that a good level of thinking is important, and many times, too little thinking is irresponsible. The key is to strike a balance; focus on what you want to accomplish and when it needs to be done.

In short, be results oriented. Establish goals for yourself and your organization. Then decide when those things should be accomplished. As you go through the process, begin collecting information so that you can make intelligent decisions as your timeline allows. Employ the advice of your experts in the effort.

On information gathering, set limits for the length of collection. Also set standards about the quality of sources from which the information will be drawn.

Next, begin the analysis, and use your instincts to navigate through the options. Make the decision, and move on. Will everything go as planned? Not always. But don't use that as an excuse to delay action.

Here's a great way to overcome blockades that impede forward movement from nature itself, water. Water is fluid and always finds a way. Water going downstream doesn't stop. When water meets an object, water embraces it. Water develops tremendous momentum as it flows, and when it meets a blockade, water either goes around, goes over, or goes through the object, or it removes the blockade. This is a great analogy on what to do when one meets obstacles along the way. As water keeps moving, so our thinking and decision making must also do the same.

Remember, don't get paralyzed by analysis. Keep in mind that the best medicine against fear, disappointment, or lack of progress is to take action. Think it through, overcome obstacles, and act expediently!

Notes

1. Roger E. Bohn and James E. Short, *How Much Information? 2009 Report on American Consumers.* (LaJolla: Global National Institute of Standards & Technology | Information Industry Center, University of California–San Diego, 2010), http://hmi.uscd.edu/howmuchinfo.php.

Chapter 21

Do the Trick: Troubleshoot before Attempting Repair

The temptation to jump right into a fix is always attractive. Resist it!

Effective personal or organizational leadership is process-oriented. When making decisions, I suggest you also be process-oriented. Do the trick!

I actually want to say TRC. So from here on out, I will write TRC, but I want you to read it as "trick." Are you with me? Good! Let's continue our journey.

TRC stands for troubleshoot, repair, and calibrate. I have been in this TRC business for a long time. My journey started in the Air Force Metrology and Calibration Program as a Precision Measurement Equipment Laboratory (PMEL) technician.

Although I don't currently calibrate as a technician, I still find myself calibrating in different organizations and my own personal life. My journey has taught me that leaders who use the TRC process are effective. Those who do not end up crushing their organizations. Let me explain. But first you need to have some background information.

A PMEL technician troubleshoots, repairs, and calibrates. He or she ensures the accuracy and reliability of weapon systems and any other system or tool used to make quantitative measurements.

Calibration is about comparing an object or thing to a standard and ensuring repeatable measurement accuracy in the process. PMEL technicians certify that a piece of equipment has been tested and that it demonstrates measureable, reliable functioning against precise criteria. There is a process for that. And as I walk you through that process, please think about how it applies to you as a leader.

We can draw many analogies from this process, so think of them as we go along. For example, a customer can be anyone who is asking for services from you: son, daughter, subordinate, another organization, and so forth. Equipment can be a process or person. The malfunction can be anything described as an opportunity for improvement or problem to be solved.

Here is a "bird's eye view" of the process. Customers bring equipment to the PMEL for calibration. If the equipment is functioning properly, we calibrate it. Other times, customers notice (or we would notice) malfunctions or that the equipment was just broken. Restoring the equipment to operational capability requires a TRC approach. Find the root cause of the problem before attempting a repair.

Let me note here that this process must be done in the right order. Before going straight into the repair, we troubleshoot. Troubleshooting helps you avoid costly redos. I remember repairing components with a singular cost of over $24,000. Imagine how expensive it would be to fix something quickly (for the sake of time or lack of patience) only to find out the problem was something else?

In our leadership roles, we deal with people and systems. As self, mother, father, CEO, sergeant, officer, and so forth, there is no telling how much more expensive attempting to make course corrections would be without understanding why a person, organization, or system needs fixing.

The point here is to find the root cause of the problem before attempting a repair. Listen, research, and ask the right questions; be curious. Once you've done that, sit and think about possible courses of action.

Repairs Are Not Done Arbitrarily; They Must Conform to Some Blueprint

Once the reason for the malfunction is found, the equipment is ready for repair. The manuals will tell us how the equipment is designed, and that will dictate the best approach to use. When attempting a repair, the intent is to have a clear, intended purpose in mind and understand how the thing is built. Have a clear vision of how your organization or system should work. Then apply the right method. Use tact when appropriate; involve key players—care for all. The right attitude will help you find a way.

Your Work Is Not Done until You Calibrate and Certify

Repaired equipment is now ready for testing. How? Calibrate! You compare performance output against a standard. After testing specific outputs, we certify whether or not the equipment is fully capable. If it is not, we make adjustments until the outputs meet desired results.

The goal is to understand how you are measuring up to the success you deserve. As we look at all of our life's activities, if all the systems are in place and operational, then it is time to calibrate. Compare your results against your vision. If you're not hitting the mark, make adjustments by aligning personnel, processes, and activities to achieve the desired results. Move appropriate resources and time appropriately.

This TRC process works! In whatever you do, think about when and how you can use TRCs. Are there activities you can apply this to? Of course! Give it a try. Use TRC to craft your journey.

Chapter 22

What's Really Important?

There is no way everything is highly important. Break through the fog! Otherwise, nothing will get done.

Sometimes we're busy, and other times we tell ourselves we're busy. Then, we meet with friends and we talk about who's busier. "Man, I've been so busy." "Me too—busier! Look, I was doing this and then that, plus I had to ____." (Get ready for the "Who's Really Busy" game show!) We all have been guilty of that type of behavior at one point or another. The problem is that we completely lose focus of what's important. We're out of control!

I bet if we stopped people around the community and asked, "Tell me, what's really important to you? And what do you think will be important in your future?" people will go blank more often than not. And for those who are quick to respond, if we followed up with another question, "So how much time do you spend on this thing you mentioned as important?" most of the time, the person would merely stare, unable to comprehend or even realize the misalignment of priorities.

For some people, like me, who "keep going and going" all day like the Energizer Bunny, we are in danger. We may be living a life of deception, thinking we are achieving, producing results. And who knows? This may be true, but the danger stems from trying to do so much that we can no longer recognize what's urgent, what's important, what's trivial, and what's waste. Remember, this is similar to finding ourselves out of control. So stop for a second. As I have said elsewhere, "Ask yourself, 'What are the activities that will produce the most bang for the investment in time and resources?' Work on those first!"[1]

Staying busy is a good thing. But staying busy doing the right things is much better! Time management? Forget it! You cannot manage time. You only have 24 hours in a day. You can't produce another hour.

In his book *The 7 Habits of Highly Effective People*, Dr. Stephen R. Covey makes a good point about great people and great leaders. Great people, great leaders, practice the habit of "first things first."[2] In short, they break through the fog and chaos by giving their lives clarity. How? Great leaders make clear what's important to them and their organizations. Then they analyze each of the activities they're doing and decide, based on clear priorities, what will be done first.

One key ingredient, as Dr. Covey puts it, is to be able to decipher between what's important and what appears to be important. Then do the important first and say no to the unimportant. Sometimes what appears to be urgent is not important. But when one creates the habit of responding to urgency without an analysis of the task's contribution to a worthy objective, one begins to veer out of control.

The product of "urgency reaction" is the complaint about not having enough time. Even more dangerous is the possibility that the truly important will not get done, or when done, quality will suffer.

So what's really important? One way to answer that question is to ask yourself, "If I had a month left to live, on what activities would I concentrate? What would be the things I would circle on a piece of paper as my legacy?"

Another way to answer the question is to ask yourself, "Do I have a motto for life?" My motto is, "I live by the 5 Fs" (Faith, Family, Fitness, Flag, and Friends). Then, I evaluate if I have done anything in the month in relation to each of the Fs.

Whatever you decide to use, just do it. Decide what is important to you in your specific area of responsibility, then break through the fog and give your situation clarity. Adopt a motto for life and live by it. Be GREAT!

Notes

1. Jose A. Lugo Santiago, "Pareto Eyeglasses—Learning to See," *Jose LugoSantiago—Craft Your Journey!* (blog), 24 March 2014, http://www.joselugosantiago.com/lead-inspire/pareto-eyeglasses-learning-to-see.

2. Stephen R. Covey, *The 7 Habits of Highly Effective People: Restoring the Character Ethic* (New York: Free Press, 2004).

Part 4

Dealing with Teamwork on your Leadership Journey

I don't know what your destiny will be, but one thing I do know: the only ones among you who will be really happy are those who have sought and found how to serve.

—Albert Schweitzer

If you can't produce teamwork, you're not a leader. We can spend days talking about the education you have, the people you supervise, and the position you hold. Still, you will not convince me. The very nature of leadership demands that your relationship with people and your influence becomes a powerful force that propels and inspires them to action.

Leaders accomplish work through the employment of teams. Therefore, if you want to be a great leader, you must learn to serve and work within, and with, teams.

These conversations are reflections on team performance. I've worked, formed, led, and continue to lead a diverse set of teams in diverse settings. This is all "battle" tested. Let's talk!

Chapter 23

Can You Teach Me?

If we expect our children to be learners, we, too, should expect ourselves to be learners.

Have you ever met a person who knew it all? All of us, at one point or another, may have felt we've met one of those people. And we might have said, "I hope I don't turn out that way!" Let me assure you I am not talking about dismissing personal convictions or the assertion that each of us has gifts developed over a lifetime. I am talking about attitude. Let me dive into a short example.

You have an important task to accomplish. You call a meeting and put the team in a room to discuss the task. The discussion begins, and the team members start brainstorming ideas. As they discuss, you start picking at every brainstormed idea—you're not supposed to do that! Remember, it's a brainstorming session! Anyway, you tell your team, "When I ____." Followed by, "Last year, I ____." Then another, "When I served on the commission for ____." Again, this may be necessary, but when you assume an attitude where there is no room for learning or trying something new because you've seen it all, then everyone loses.

As leaders, we have to be conscious of how our expertise can hinder the performance of teams. We must also acknowledge that we truly don't know it all. Our expertise needs to be refreshed. Therefore, we must be constant learners. As Benjamin Franklin opined, "Being ignorant is not so much a shame, as being unwilling to learn."

Regardless of the leadership role (mom, dad, organizational leader, sports coach, and so forth), everyone has an important need to continue developing. It's important that you acknowledge your gifts and offer your expertise. And as you do that, be prepared to learn and refresh.

Here are some helpful hints:

- **Listen**. It may sound cliché, but here is a powerful thought: "That's why we have two ears and one mouth—to listen twice as much as we speak." There is a lot of wisdom in that. Listen to what is said without judgment. Reflect. If you really want to test your understanding, repeat to the person you're listening to what you just heard. Have the person make the necessary corrections so that you know the message was received as intended. No, it's not easy. But if you make it a habit, you'll greatly improve your relationship with team members.

- **Question your assertions**. We don't always have the entire story. Mesh your experience with what you're hearing and begin to ask yourself, "Where are my knowledge gaps?"
- **Be flexible**. Overcome your own biases and be ready to learn. If you want to be effective in helping those around you and truly make meaningful changes in your life, you cannot be too prideful. Our own successes sometimes get in the way. If you have been successful doing X, then it's hard to accept that doing Y can make you more successful. Temper everything with good judgment and be ready to change if needed.
- **Read**. You should maintain a yearly reading plan. Read about two or three books about your areas of expertise. Then, read one or two books about something else. For example, if you always read leadership books, pick up a science fiction book for your next read.

Leaders are lifelong learners. Learning will keep your mind and body healthy. Learning will spark innovation and energy. Do it. In improving your learning ability, always ask, "So what can I learn today?"

Chapter 24

E-mail Warrior?

E-mail needs to be managed or it will cost you. Use it with artistic strategy.

I am not trying to wage a war against e-mail, but certain behaviors in aspiring leaders trouble me. Although I applaud the usefulness of e-mail as a superb tool, in my leader's mind, e-mail is not communication. E-mail, of course, plays a crucial part in the communication loop, though. My worry and my thought in this conversation stem from my observations about "e-mail leadership." Do you know what I mean?

Let me give you some examples. I build and work with teams to accomplish countless projects. Some projects are long term; others are short term. The good majority of these projects require people to come together, discuss issues, and brainstorm solutions. Ultimately, those teams must execute for success. So in meetings with those teams, I find myself checking on projects' progress and assessing team effectiveness. Not so long ago, we were zeroing in on a project. I asked several questions.

Me: "Is Agency-X involved in this project?"

Answer: "Yes, we have communicated with the agency and got a response."

Me: "What do you mean with 'communicated,' because I have not heard or seen anything from that organization?"

Answer: "Well, we sent them an e-mail, and Mrs. Jones from Agency-X said she was going to work that for us."

Me: "E-mail? If you're not getting results, did you actually pick up the phone or walk, drive, or bike to that organization to see if they're still there?"

And on other occasions where we were trying to promote projects—and the response was less than stellar—I heard answers similar to this one: "Well, we've sent lots of e-mails and have advertised in the ____ but we're not getting the response."

Throughout my career, I have seen the reliance on e-mail develop to the point of self-deception. We begin to believe e-mail is the injection that will cure inaction. And in so believing, we sail away from the basic principal that human contact produces magic! Human contact makes the miracles happen—we just can't forget that.

All of us, as leaders, need to approach e-mail leadership with great caution. E-mail has a huge price tag associated with it. Let me give you an example of what I mean.

Concerned about productivity in my organization, I went on a search for answers. (I blame this sense of curiosity on my lean/six sigma black-belt instincts!) So I decided to dive deeper into the issue of e-mail. Senior corporate executives get a lot of e-mail. As a matter of fact, in 2011 national statistics showed that corporate executives sent and received about 105 e-mails per day.[1] I am one of those statistics, with a count of about 120 e-mails a day.

Here's a quick glance of what I found in my organization. In 2012 we had about 18,000 users, sending about 350,000 e-mails per day. When I took into consideration the average number of e-mails we sent per day, time in typing, minimum salary wages, and multiplied that by the months in a year, the amount of resources invested were in the billions of dollars.

Another statistic not always fully explored is the cost in processing e-mails. As we all know, employees have to sort through them, read them, think through the answers, and then type the answers. Did I mention follow-up on those e-mails? Consider that many times those e-mails become the source of misunderstanding and conflict among departments. Then, as leaders, we all have to spend time dealing with those situations. When I estimated the cost of those actions in my organization, the cost was close to a quarter of a billion dollars. These were all conservative estimates.

Now, factor that cost into your budget at a time when resources have dried out. You probably can't afford it. The point here is that e-mail needs to be managed, or it will cost you.

In the project dialogue with my team (presented at the beginning of this conversation), I knew e-mail was costing me resources: wait time, extra labor from follow-up actions, misinterpretations of sender and receiver meaning, conflict resolution between parties in an e-mail conversation, and more!

My expectation for team members became simple: they were to become foot soldiers and face the people they were charged with leading. My expectation was for them to call those organizations who were stakeholders, show the importance of their contribution, and then close the loop with e-mail.

E-mail is best when used with artistic strategy. If we want results in our endeavors, whatever that might be, let us first discover the magic that exists in the people-to-people relations.

Get out of the office or home and visit the person with whom you need to do business. Use the phone. Then, send an e-mail to close the loop. And then thank the person for his or her precious time! Human contact makes miracles happen.

Notes

1. Sara Radicati, ed., and Quoc Hoang, *Email Statistics Report, 2011–2015* (Palo Alto, CA: Radicati Group, May 2011), 3, http://www.radicati.com/?p=7261.

Chapter 25

My Lego Robot

The most important single ingredient in the formula of success is knowing how to get along with people.

—Pres. Theodore Roosevelt

On a Friday night, I sat down with my young son before he went to bed. I asked him to talk to me about the good and the not so good things in his day.

He told me, "Well, we had our Lego robot class today."

Excitedly, I asked him, "Wow, that's great, son! So how did it go?!"

My son responded without excitement, "Uhmm—not so good."

"Why son, what went wrong?" I asked.

"Papa, the other kids and I could not decide on the parts. We could not stop arguing. Our team definitely did not do a good job."

"And then, what happened, son?" I prompted him, so I could get the rest of the story.

He went on, "Well, the teacher came back, took our design, disassembled it, and built something else for us to finish next week. None of us like that robot."

I looked at him, took a deep breath, and immediately thought about how similar this situation is to our adult world. You know what I mean?

Many times we have teammates with great ideas. Other times, we have some amazing ideas. And we are charged with accomplishing a project, but the ultimate miracle—the birth of something magnificent, like building that robot—does not come to fruition because members on the team (even ourselves) can't let go of their own individual thinking and open their minds to something new.

And then, someone else takes over the project, and from that point forward it's dictatorial leadership. We don't like it, but truth be told, we put ourselves in that position. Our inability to get along, to put aside differences, and to see the insights in differing points of view lead us to ruin. In our leadership roles, we cannot abide situations like the one just described.

Easier said than done, I know! What can we do? When I talked with my young son about his situation, I asked for some suggestions about how he could help the situation in the future. I pondered his thoughts and my experiences in solving conflicts to move projects forward. Here are some thoughts on getting along, to help us in difficult moments:

- **Love your people**. Every person on your team is valuable. It's important to acknowledge their capacities. Understand that cognitive diversity adds a serious dimensional lead to organizational performance.
- **Focus on the task**. Explain to your team what is to be accomplished. Trust me, this is not always self-evident. As you focus on the task, watch the team dynamics.
- **Shape the environment**. Allow everyone to embrace an attitude of "greater good." Shaping the environment will require you to be an effective communicator. Speak with passion and purpose. Everything that is done on that project should focus on that greater good, the ultimate purpose, which is greater than any single person. It's about making a miracle happen. And that requires everyone's selfless service.
- **Be strong, be and think positive, and be persistent**. All of us need to watch our interactions. Does our behavior invite or divide? Make the corrections. When you don't believe you're the cause of the friction, be proactive and be the person to reach out to amend the situation when needed. This, in fact, is the true sign of a strong and resilient person. Resilient people are able to reach to others. They also understand that behind each mountain, beautiful valleys exist, awaiting discovery. That's why strong and resilient people don't give up.

In dealing with diverse sets of teams, cultures, and personalities, I've found these four steps on getting along form the right formula for success. Add them to your repertoire. As you facilitate team performance, you will improve your team's power to finish whatever Lego robot project comes their way!

Chapter 26

The Ground Crew

Before you are a leader, success is all about growing yourself. When you become a leader, success is all about growing others.

—Jack Welch

In early October 2013, I visited the Smithsonian's National Air and Space Museum in Washington DC. It's impressive! Did you know the museum holds the world's largest and most-significant collection of aviation and space artifacts? Its collections incorporate the entire history of human flight.

As you enter the foyer, in the main entrance of the museum, one can see a prominent display of aircraft and rockets hanging from the ceiling and even an astronaut representing our journey into space. We've come so far as a human race in such a short aviation history.

As I observed all of the machinery and displays, I felt quiet in my thoughts. I was transported for a brief moment to Ramstein Air Base, Germany, where I served in the early 1990s and then again in the early 2000s. I led over 400 very motivated Airmen, responsible for the maintenance of aircraft.

The time came when one of our aircraft needed to be readied for an important mission. The selected aircraft went through an extensive inspection. It was first washed. Then, the maintenance crews disassembled sections of the aircraft, engines, and parts of the fuselage and then put the plane together again. When all was done, it was a beautiful fully mission-capable air machine.

We then made a phone call to announce to our next command echelon that the aircraft was ready for the general to fly. I lined up the maintenance crews on the flight line and waited. The general arrived. I called the formation to attention and saluted.

"Good morning, Sir! The aircraft is ready for your inspection and flight." The general saluted, patted me on the shoulder, and greeted everyone. One of my youngest crew chiefs walked around the aircraft with the general.

The general taxied the aircraft down the flight line and took off into the air. While flying, he circled back to where we were formed up. He saluted us and continued the flight.

We were there waiting for him when he landed. So I asked him, "Sir, do you always circle back? I hear you do that almost every time."

He said, "Yes I do. That's my way to say thank you for the privilege of flying. You see, without your young Airmen, we would not be able to fly."

I considered those words very wise back then, and they're still true today. If you are a leader in your organization, you're the pilot in this example. The organization is your aircraft, and people accomplishing the daily tasks of the mission (entrusted to you) are the the ground crews.

One should never underestimate the importance of a world-class "ground crew." I am talking about appreciating people who are committed to the organization and high standards and who go the extra mile when needed. Their work allows us the privilege of flying.

You, the leader, are responsible to the next echelon but also to the ground crew. Imagine what would happen if your ground crew lacked the tools to do their jobs? And if you've made sure the tools are available, imagine if you've not spent time ensuring "disciplined maintenance" is a natural culture in your organization? Can you then fly? And if you're flying, will the aircraft stay together in flight?

Many times, leaders get caught up in the "business" of the day. Days go by without leaders circling back to see how the ground crews are doing. Break that cycle!

Start by modeling the energy, attitude, and commitment you want to see in your ground crew. Communicate clearly, both verbally and in writing, expectations of conduct and performance. Evaluate crew performance. Hold the line on standards. Give feedback and get directly involved to close knowledge and empowerment gaps.

And don't forget to publicly show your confidence in your crew. Circle back as you're flying in your daily affairs, and thank your ground crew for the privilege of flying!

Chapter 27

Helping Each Other

The scarcity mentality ruins us. Stop thinking poor thoughts and begin thinking abundantly. Then, we will find abundance.

On the first week of March 2013, millions of Americans were glued to newscasts, awaiting resolution on the big question of sequestration. Here is one of the headlines that morning from *NBC News*: "Frustration Aimed at Washington over Sequester: The Sequester Likely Won't Be the Doomsday Scenario Some Predicted, as the Cuts Will Kick in Gradually, but There Is Public Frustration at Washington for Not Doing More, Sooner."

Any one of us could look at that situation and begin to unravel it with myriad conclusions, assertions, and thoughts. I don't want to dive into any of them. I just want to look at the situation and bring it to our own leadership experience in dealing with teams and families and in accomplishing what's important.

Bringing that situation—the deadlock and lack of progress on issues that created public frustration—to our own unique leadership settings in our workplaces, we have to ask ourselves several questions:

- With so much self-interest among workplace participants, how can I help build a sense of unity and teamwork?
- How can I help someone else accomplish their goals, while at the same time gaining another person's commitment to help me accomplish my goals? and
- Can I facilitate people and/or organizations focusing their external and internal interests on the greater good?

Those questions suggest there is a place where everyone can win. And my leadership experience tells me such a place exists. That place is a point of balance and high performance: the fulcrum. On either side of the fulcrum, there is a combination of lose-lose and lose-win thinking. No one really wins if we, as leaders, operate on either side of the fulcrum because either you or your team members may be distracted by the possibility that someone can lose. Great leaders must strive to bring everyone to think about fulcrum balance.

Achieving fulcrum balance can be done. We just have to change how we think. We need to begin thinking win-win and then get ready for the tough road ahead. This necessitates emotional toughness and intelligence. One has to turn problems into opportunities.

When you see conflict in your environment, how is it resolved? Does one person win, and the other one lose? I bet the reason, in many instances, for the deadlock and lack of progress on issues (just like the situation in the headlines) is because we cannot let go of a mentality that promotes scarcity (someone wins and another one loses).

Let go of scarcity thoughts. If you are the leader of a team or family and think poor thoughts, you will have a poor team or family. The contrary is also true. If you have thoughts of abundance, you will end up with abundance in your team and/or family. As civil rights leader Edgar Daniel Nixon opined, "Your spark can become a flame and change everything."

Creating abundance starts with several actions. First, watch your thoughts. Go into every situation understanding that a "let's help each other" mind-set is an overwhelming source of energy that most likely can yield positive results for everyone. Express that vision, and let everyone see and feel the beauty of crafting a vision where everyone wins.

Leaders who can inspire a common sentiment (a win-win, abundance mentality) reach higher and push the team higher in accomplishments. Those leaders can inspire others because they stop focusing on what they want and begin focusing on what others need. Importantly, leaders inspire others because their focus is external. The focus is outward. This type of leadership creates abundance.

A second important action in creating abundance deals with your biases. Be aware of your biases: they drive your behaviors. Your thoughts and actions should build an atmosphere where everyone wants to help each other.

In a conversation with executive coach Pamela Corbett, she mentioned to me something I thought was profound in dealing with biases, emotions, and behaviors:

How you interpret an experience, or the value that you attach to it, is what shapes your reaction. Different people can have the same experience but report very different emotional reactions. What varies is the person and how they interpret the experience. So when confronted with an awkward experience, you need to ask yourself, how else can I look at it? Change your perspective, and you change how you feel.[1]

Lastly, in creating an abundance, win-win mind-set, forget who takes the credit. Your aim is to build partnerships and achieve richness for everyone. Who gets credit for the success doesn't matter.

Imagine how much more the team could achieve if no one on the team cares about who gets the credit! In the end, if everyone comes together thinking win-win and abundance for all, your team will achieve results that never seemed possible.

Remember, the best way to help each other is to throw away the scarcity mentality and welcome a mentality of abundance. Abundant thoughts lead to abundant team performance.

Notes

1. Pamela Corbett, neurolinguistic programming master practitioner, executive coach, and leadership development expert, telephone interview by author, 14 February 2013.

Chapter 28

Leading Generations, Part 1

Today's workforce is the most diverse in American history. What a blessing! Leaders, now more than ever, must employ leadership art to motivate and inspire.

Today is one of the most interesting times of all ages. It's perhaps one of the most challenging times also. The big challenge comes in making decisions that produce strong collaboration among all the members of a very diverse workforce. Keep in mind that the aim of the leader, while he or she leads that diverse workforce, is to facilitate high performance and build an enjoyable work environment that nurtures the growth of the organization and its people. That's not an easy feat!

So there you are, in a meeting, trying to figure out the best quality of life initiatives for your workforce. Your bias toward a younger generation may make you assume they need expensive gadgets to get the job done or to communicate better. Your own bias may make you decide on the "best" expenditure—only to later find out the buy was a waste and not well received by a good part of your workforce.

The same goes when you lead older employees. You may think they want this or that because of your management studies or because your own parents behaved that way. You may risk instituting workplace rewards that are appealing to you but are meaningless to older workers.

Leaders have many reasons to be concerned about providing good leadership to this workforce. Many scholars speak about this workforce as the most diverse we've ever had. Many of us are aware of these facts, but when it comes down to the actual awareness during the day's leadership journey, many of us forget how these differences in generations affect our decisions and behaviors.

Leading without the awareness of generational differences creates leadership self-deceptive boxes. The leader may think he or she is making all the right decisions but can't comprehend why the people in the work center continue to be unhappy and/or don't get along. I have seen that frustration in leaders many times.

The first step in avoiding self-deceptive boxes is awareness. What generations are we dealing with and "who" are they? I have pondered this question. I have studied the generational changes and have talked about this topic in leadership talks. Every time, my research in this area points me to new discoveries. In short, the volume of information is huge.

Here is a surface look at this complex universe to give you foundational knowledge and empower your awareness as you deal with the generational diversity of teams. Although four generations exist, the last three generations are by far the most prevalent in today's workforce, and those will be the focus of our discussion. The four generations are the Silents, Baby Boomers, Generation X, and Millenials. Let's talk about the last three briefly:

- **Baby Boomers (born between 1946 and 1964).** This generation experienced significant life-changing events that shaped its values system. The American Management Association named key events that led to the shaping of boomers' values system. For example, the boomers experienced social revolution of the 1960s, the Vietnam War, the assassination of prominent leaders (Pres. John F. Kennedy, Dr. Martin Luther King Jr., and others), saw the first landing on the moon, and were assimilated into the workforce during a period of high inflation that lasted nearly two decades between 1965 and 1982. The role of television played a substantial role in their society. Some scholars also labeled this generation the "workaholics" because they were driven, optimistic, highly competitive micromanagers, irritated by lazy employees, declaring a higher priority for work over personal life. With regard to work, boomers lived by the credo of "don't leave for tomorrow what you can do today."[1]

- **Generation X (born between 1965 and 1980).** This generation grew up with both parents in the workforce or in households where parents were divorced. As a result, this generation became more independent at a younger age. Experts say Xers experienced social insecurity and a lack of solid traditions.[2] Members of this generation disliked the attitude of their parents and grew up skeptical of the loyalty parents had to their employers who kept parents out of balance with the needs of families. For this reason, Xers grew up seeing the need for relationships and families as much a priority as the needs of employers. Generation X created a different philosophy of living: the work-life balance.[3] Preceding generations labeled Generation X as one that complained too much and was cynical and unmotivated. Others termed Xers as the "slacker" generation for its insistence on making life-balance more important than the work-centric life of other generations.[4] Xers naturally question authority figures and believe in gaining skills they can take to other institutions.[5] Such behavior has made this generation technically stronger and more independent than prior generations. Interestingly, this generation entered the workforce competing with the Baby Boomers.

- **Millennials or Generation Ys (born after 1980)**. This is perhaps the most misunderstood generation in the workplace for leaders today. Millennials' core beliefs are shaped by substantial change. This generation has seen more life-changing events early in their lives than all the other preceding generations: the fall of the Berlin Wall, integration of MTV in their lives, high school shootings, frequent natural disasters, and terrorist attacks.[6] Some call this generation, the "Internet" generation. Growing in an environment where the Internet has made global reach possible and where global terrorist threats have increased, this generation is the first one deemed as global-centric. They are also considered among the most resilient in navigating change and most appreciative of diversity and inclusion. They are also the most educated generation of workers we have in the workplace right now.[7]

By now, you have a good understanding of who these generations are. Let's talk about what's important to them:

- **Baby Boomers**. Of course, this generation feels they've worked very hard and have put in the long hours, so rewards for them derive from their status: money, title, seniority, the corner office, and any other indicators that would let anyone know their standing among others.[8] They want to be known as experts and feel their years of experience and knowledge should be valued and rewarded.[9] Working important projects that would cause societal change is also motivating to them. One recent change in the priorities of this generation is the gradual shift from the value of money to the value of time, especially as they get older.[10]

- **Generation X.** This generation saw their parents tangled in the corporate web with little time for anything else. Freedom and flexibility for the Xers is the ultimate reward, as they strive to achieve work-life balance.[11] At work, they prefer immediate feedback as a form of knowing how well their doing. As a matter of fact, Lancaster & Stillman explained that in multiple surveys 90 percent of Xers responded they wanted feedback immediately or within a few days after completing a project.[12] They feel the work world is filled with uncertainty, so rewards come from those things that can be portable like building new skill sets they can take with them wherever they go.[13] Even their attitude toward retirement compensation is one of "best if I can take it with me." According to the American Management Association, this generation was the first one to prepare for retirement without Social Security.[14]

- **Millennials or Generation Ys.** This generation works well in teams and seeks collaboration.[15] Millennials are also considered results oriented and demonstrate tremendous performance endurance under pressure.[16] In their professional careers, millennials expect to change jobs often, so tangible and intangible rewards are important to them. Some examples of tangible rewards include tickets to events and discounts at retail stores—things they can cash in now and brag to their friends about later. Being able to participate in decision making, having bosses who relate to them, working in teams, and being engaged in work that has meaning are important intangible rewards.[17] They are good at multitasking but expect clear direction, without micromanaging. Achieving work-life balance is also important for millennials. If they cannot get the work-life flexibility they want in the workplace, they'll seek somewhere else where they can get it.[18]

As you will be leading these generations, hopefully, this conversation helps you think about yourself and others in your work environment. Let me caveat the end of this part of our conversation with a caution. Although it may be easy to stereotype, don't. Use this conversation only as a point of reference to understand how social change has shaped the generations with which you work. Remember, having these generations present in your work center makes your workforce diverse, and that is truly a blessing.

Take a break from reading. Let it sink in. Don't proceed to our next conversation until tomorrow. We'll then continue the second part of this conversation. See you then!

Notes

1. Ian N. Bradford and Patrick T. Hester, *Analysis of Generation Y Workforce Motivation Using Multi-attribute Utility Theory* (Fort Belvoir, VA: Defense Acquisition University, 2011), 65–72.
2. Ibid., 65.
3. "The Clash of the Generations," *US Department of Labor Women's Bureau E-News*, 13 August 2008, http://www.dol.gov/wb/media/newsletter/e-news15artl-02.htm.
4. Geoffrey Paulin and Brian Riordon, "Making It on Their Own: The Baby Boom Meets Generation X," *Monthly Labor Review*, February 1998, 10–21, http://www.bls.gov/mlr/1998/02/art2full.pdf.
5. American Management Association, "Leading the Four Generations at Work," 11 June 2014, http://www.amanet.org/training/articles/Leading-the-Four-Generations-at-Work.aspx.
6. Bradford and Hester, *Analysis of Generation Y Workforce*, 67.
7. American Management Association, "Leading the Four Generations."
8. Lynne C. Lancaster and David Stillman, "From a Gold Clock to Founder's Stock: Rewarding the Generations," in *When Generations Collide: Who They Are, Why They Clash, How to Solve the Generational Puzzle at Work* (New York: HarperCollins, 2009), 82.
9. "The Clash of the Generations."
10. Lancaster and Stillman, "From a Gold Clock to Founder's Stock," 87.
11. Ibid., 82.
12. Ibid., 224.
13. "The Clash of the Generations."
14. American Management Association, "Leading the Four Generations."
15. Ibid.
16. Bradford and Hester, *Analysis of Generation Y Workforce*, 67.
17. Lancaster and Stillman, "From a Gold Clock to Founder's Stock," 82.
18. "The Clash of the Generations."

Chapter 29

Leading Generations, Part 2

You don't lead by pointing and telling people some place to go. You lead by going to that place and making a case.

—Ken Kasey

Welcome back! In the last conversation, we focused on understanding the three prevalent generations in our workplace. Specifically, we discussed who they are, how they are different from each other, and what they value most.

Since we are now armed with that understanding, we are ready to dive into the second part of the conversation: how do we lead in this multigenerational environment and avoid self-deception? Every leader, regardless of the leadership setting (parent, supervisor, CEO, world leader, or so forth), should be concerned with the answer to this question.

Has this ever happened to you as a leader? You delivered clear project objectives and the way forward. Then, you called a meeting to check progress and found out the team went "column-half-left" on the project. They veered off from your direction. You may have taken a deep breath and told yourself, "This is not what I asked for!"

In your mind you had this magnificent picture, and of course, it was articulated perfectly, right? Well, somehow it got fuzzy in translation. That happens often in multigenerational teams. That's because the world looks different to each of the team members.

We all have experiences, backgrounds, and upbringings that are different. And all of those differences are compounded by decades of past world events, which can instill in us strong emotional labels that influence how we experience the world in the present. It's no wonder that each of the generations perceives our message in a different way.

When leading multigenerational teams, leaders must multicommunicate. Our message has to hit the hearts of our people through every word, through every written piece of correspondence, and most importantly, through every action.

Take proactive steps to avoid self-deception and improve communication, acceptance, and synergistic relationships across your multi-generational workforce. Here are a few of those steps.

Take a look at yourself first. Where do you fall in the generational continuum? This is important because people communicate based on their generational backgrounds. This awareness will help you better estimate your own biases and communication patterns and will point you to areas where you have to make adjustments or simply provide more emphasis. Greg Hammill of Fairleigh Dickinson University illustrates this point:

> When a Boomer says to another Boomer, "We need to get the report done," it is generally interpreted by the Boomer as an order[;] it must be done and done now. However, when a Boomer says to an Xer, "This needs to be done," the Xer hears an observation, not a command, and may or may not do it immediately.[1]

One must admit, this scenario is possible in any work center and drives supervisors to think the young man or woman does not care.

Secondly, take a look at how you organize work and your expectations about how work should be accomplished. Many supervisors spend inordinate amounts of time dictating how work should be done. Sometimes, that is necessary; many times, it is not. The overuse of that method destroys creativity and makes people unhappy, especially Xers and millennials who seek flexibility and freedom to get their jobs done. A better approach is to let the experts work the details, and you, as the leader, spend most of your time articulating clear intent statements.

On this last point, let me emphasize, that as a leader in the organization, you should focus on the results employees must produce rather than on how they get it done. Invest in articulating a clear result, the purpose, the resources available, and clear timelines for whatever "mission" you're entrusting to your team. Don't violate this principle. Otherwise, your people will stop taking the initiative to improve organizational processes. Worse, it may kill their creativity. They will just sit around and wait for the next set of orders. In essence, think thoroughly and articulate the end result.

Third, "toss the routines." Arrange and design work activities to be exciting. This process begins with making the work-task meaningful by explaining how the task contributes to a defined purpose, even if the task is not too fancy. This has to be clear from the onset of delegating the assignment. This is powerful stuff! Let me give you a quick example of what I mean.

> One April afternoon I remember leaving work late and seeing a young Airman sweeping, by broom, a huge parking lot. I stopped the Airman and asked him, "Young man, why are you doing this by broom?" Pointing to his parked sweeper-truck, I continued asking, "Don't you want to use that?!"
>
> He then answered, "Chief, the sweeper is too big, and I can't get these corners [with it]. I can only get them by using this big broom."
>
> I was impressed! This was a huge parking lot, and the young Airman had already been working several hours. He could have cut corners, and who would have known?
>
> So then I asked two other big questions, "Why are you putting so much effort into it? What's the real reason?"
>
> He said, "Chief, my boss told me some important people are coming to this building tomorrow, so I want to make sure all is tidy around here."
>
> I quickly asked, "Who's visiting?" He really did not know. Little did he realize some of the most powerful people in the Department of Defense were going to be visiting. But he knew one thing: his job was critical to an important mission, and slacking on it would have resulted in a bad first impression.

Another noteworthy item in making work activities exciting is proper managing and control of meetings. Meetings can drain the energy out of people and consume the little time you have left. In much research, experts conclude that millennials and Xers dislike the formality of regular meetings, especially when there's nothing to discuss. Some meetings are important. Limit meetings for when there's a real need.

Lastly, another step leaders can take in managing a multigenerational workforce is to provide a good cross-flow of communication. In my experience, a good mentorship program where older employees teach (or learn from) younger ones and vice-versa across a diverse set of tasks, can be a critical part of cross-flow communication, facilitating team integration.

The above actions are, of course, not all inclusive, but it's a solid start. These actions will help you keep the workforce engaged, integrated, growing, and learning.

The rest is about you as a leader. Take a sincere interest in your people. When friction occurs, be prompt to respond to those needs;

facilitate problem solving and conflict resolution. Notice I did not say you will be the one solving the problem. Let the team members do it. Your role on the team is to facilitate problem solving. Use the talents of this amazing multigenerational workforce. We're truly blessed to be beneficiaries of this kind of diversity!

Notes

1. Greg Hammill, "Mixing and Managing Four Generations of Employees," *FDU Magazine*, Spring 2005, http://www.fdu.edu/newspubs/magazine/05ws/generations.htm.

Chapter 30

Building a Space Station

Leadership + Teamwork = The International Space Station. If it was possible in space, imagine what can be possible here on earth!

In 2013 I had the opportunity to visit Space Center Houston. One cannot help but be speechless when observing how far we've come as a human race. Take, for example, the International Space Station. The National Aeronautics and Space Administration (NASA) speaks of the space station as the greatest human and technological achievement.[1] How was it accomplished? Take a few moments to think about the complexities involved in that achievement.

First, it is an international partnership of space agencies. The principals come from the United States, Russia, Europe, Japan, and Canada.[2] Each of those countries has its own hardware, logistics, research, funding streams, social complexities, languages—I think you catch my drift.

Secondly, the "elements [of the space station] launched from different countries and continents are not mated together until they reach orbit, and some elements that have been launched later in the assembly sequence were not yet built when the first elements were placed in orbit."[29] That is truly a mission impossible made possible. That's inspiring—a true testament to how the impossible can also be possible here on earth.

Leaders struggle with building what sometimes seems like the International Space Station here on earth. We, as leaders, put people together from all walks of life, who have their own internal languages, biases, agendas, and so forth. Getting work accomplished or building something never before attempted can be difficult. If you find yourself in that environment, here are some tips I've found to be effective in accomplishing impossibilities:

- **Build a team.** If you have a special project, you may be able to select people. Select those who live life with passion. Pick a variety of people with varied skills—diversity wins! One of those skills should be mediation. I call those people bridge builders.

Team members, especially in the beginning stages (forming and storming stages), tend to pull in different directions. Your bridge builder will help navigate the team through difficult times.

- **Explain the task**. It is not always obvious, so don't take it for granted. In my experience, I have found that explaining the task is all about communicating your vision, the resources available, and what you do not want to see. This quote from Maj Gen Stephen Goldfein, USAF, is one of my favorite explanations of this point; its application is relevant to all leaders, regardless of leadership setting: "In the end, commanders do only two things—provide the vision and set the environment. Almost everything you do for the organization falls into one of these two categories. You will be tempted to focus elsewhere. If you do, it is likely you are performing someone else's job."[3]

- **Define clear roles**. Anytime team members are confused on who is who or who does what, the team is bound to have difficulties. Personality clashes will emerge and effort will be wasted through duplication if roles and responsibilities are unclear.

- **Follow-up**. Adopt regularly scheduled meetings with your team. Structure meetings to see accomplished work. Make sure to have a recorder and a timekeeper, so you can dedicate yourself to content. When everyone leaves, all should be clear about deliverables, action items, and follow-ups. Don't forget to thank and recognize those who overcame obstacles and produced quality work.

- **Celebrate**. Throughout the life cycle of the team, it's important to cultivate healthy relationships. One way to do this is to have social gatherings at key intervals—no agendas, just getting together. Schedule these gatherings early, so everyone can attend. Informal social gatherings do great things toward helping team members develop commitment to one another.

The rest is about being optimistic and expecting the best while monitoring outcomes. Sometimes we do not have a choice on the work that must be done, but we always have the opportunity to change how we feel about what we must do.

As the Cub Scout motto articulates "Do Your Best!" Do your best and expect the best. If the task is difficult—whatever the assigned task might be—don't worry. You too can build the space station. If it was possible in space with multination partners; it is also possible here on earth!

Notes

1. Brian Dunbar and Mark Garcia, ed., "International Cooperation," National Aeronautics and Space Administration (web site), 21 August 2015, http://www.nasa.gov/mission_pages/station/cooperation/index.html.

2. Brian Dunbar and Mark Garcia, ed., "International Partners and Participants," National Aeronautics and Space Administration (web site), 21 August 2015, http://www.nasa.gov/mission_pages/station/structure/elements/partners.html.

3. Quoted in David L. Goldfein, *Sharing Success—Owning Failure: Preparing to Command in the Twenty-First Century Air Force* (Maxwell AFB, AL: Air University Press, 2001), 23, http://www.au.af.mil/au/awc/awcgate/au/goldfein.pdf.